CHILD
WELFARE
PERSPECTIVES

Selected Papers of Joseph H. Reid

Edited by Ann W. Shyne

CHILD WELFARE LEAGUE OF AMERICA, INC.
67 Irving Place·New York, NY 10003

CHILD WELFARE LEAGUE OF AMERICA

67 Irving Place, New York, New York 10003

ISBN: 0-87868-133-7

Current printing (last digit)
10 9 8 7 6 5 4 3 2 1

PRINTED IN THE UNITED STATES OF AMERICA

CONTENTS

IV. EDUCATION AND UTILIZATION OF STAFF

INTRODUCTION

During his 28 years at the League, 25 as its executive director, Joseph Reid made innumerable speeches at meetings not only throughout the United States and Canada but in many other parts of the world. Some of these were subsequently published and appear on the roster of his publications in this book. Many were given from notes and no written record remains. But copies of many that were located merit a wider audience than those privileged to hear them.

The proposal to publish these papers, initiated by Clara J. Swan, Associate Director of Field Operations, met a warm response from Mrs. Walter B. Driscoll, President of the League, Carl Schoenberg, Director of Publications, and myself, as the suggested editor, as well as the staff. The only resistance came from Mr. Reid, who minimized the worth of his speeches and papers and was exceedingly reluctant to approve a publication that might be regarded as a personal tribute to him. Only as he was persuaded that the material articulated positions of the League that were of both historical importance and current interest and use to the field, did he withdraw his opposition to the project. In view of his attitude, we have refrained from including, as planned, a formal review and appreciation of his contributions to child welfare policy, program and practice, although we would otherwise have much to say about his leadership in child welfare in the 20th century. We confine ourselves to brief, factual data about the author.

Joseph H. Reid was born in Lima, Ohio. He earned a bachelor of arts degree and a master's degree in social work at the University of Washington. His principal experience before joining the CWLA staff in 1950 as assistant executive director was 4 years as an officer in the United States Navy and 6 years at the Ryther Child Center in Seattle. Over the last 25 years Mr. Reid has served on the board of the National Assembly of National Voluntary Health and Social Welfare Organizations, Inc., as a vice president of the Christian Children's Fund and of the American Parents Committee, as deputy president of the International Union on Child Welfare, and as a member of numerous governmental committees and commissions.

Our criteria for selection of papers were simple. Obviously, book-length publications could not be included, such as *Residential Treatment Centers for Emotionally Disturbed Children*, written with Helen R. Hagan in 1952, which served its purpose as "a base from which to evaluate and better understand clinical studies and reports from residential treatment centers." We decided to confine ourselves to papers that had not appeared in readily accessible publications. Mr. Reid's chapter "Action Called For—Recommendations," in *Children in Need of Parents*, published in 1959, is an excellent statement of the whole gamut of measures needed to counteract the problem of unnecessary continuance of children in foster care, but this should be in any social work library. "Is All Well With the American Family?", one of Mr. Reid's favorite papers, in which he stressed child welfare and other social services as essential community services necessitated by the same social forces that have created a strong industrial economy, was published in the Official Proceedings of the 1958 National Conference on Social Welfare. "Principles, Values and Assumptions Underlying Adoption Practice," a forward-looking paper of continuing relevance, appeared in *Social Work* in 1957. These are but a few of the papers that might well have been included, had they not already been within the interested reader's ready access.

Another criterion was that the papers should have more than local or transitory interest; this ruled out just a few. Also excluded were papers dealing with a highly specialized aspect of child welfare, such as "Auspices and Legal Aspects of In-Patient Psychiatric Treatment," delivered in 1956, and "Patterns of Partnership," a 1969 address strongly supportive of the role of foster parent organizations in upgrading the quality and status of foster care. We were not deterred, however, from selecting a paper solely because the exact date and occasion of its presentation could not be determined; three such inadequately documented pieces are included.

In relation to this publication, Mr. Reid wondered whether the continued timeliness of statements and recommendations made 5, 10, or 20 years ago did not imply that the League has been ineffective in accomplishing its objectives, in implementing its proposals. Mr. Reid answered this question himself nearly 20 years ago in a speech made at the League's Eastern Regional Conference in 1959, when he urged his audience not to be impatient at the apparent dearth of dramatic changes. He pointed out that such gross problems as child labor have been dealt with and large-scale gains have been made, so that the present task is to reinforce past gains and strive for limited goals that would cumulatively lead to achievement of larger ones. Progress has been made toward many of the goals articulated by Mr. Reid and other spokesmen for the League over the last 25 years, but none of those expressed in the papers presented here has been so fully achieved that it is no longer a goal today.

All too often the interests of the Child Welfare League have been erroneously identified with specific services such as foster care and adoption. The papers that follow should correct any such misperception, for the concept of child welfare that pervades them is that summarized in the following excerpt from a speech made by Mr. Reid at the 1954 National Conference of Social Work.

> The primary aim of any child welfare agency is to preserve the integrity of the family whenever possible and desirable. When difficulties arise within the family, a way is sought to preserve the ability of the family to care for its own child. Among the services specifically designed for this purpose are parent-child counseling, group and foster day care, homemaker service, visiting teacher service, protective and probationary services. Only when the nature of the family problem is such that the child cannot be cared for within his own home are foster care services brought into play. First, every effort is made to keep the child as close to normal community life as possible. A foster home is the common service used for this purpose. When the nature of the child's problems, or sometimes the family problems, is such that the child cannot live in a normal community setting, group homes and institutions are used. All of these services are, however, a means to the end of restoring the child to his own family. It is considered a basic responsibility of all children's agencies that, concomitant with and as an integral part of their service for the child cared for outside his own home, work be carried on designed to remove the obstacles to the child's living in his own home. In my view, no children's agency should be permitted to exist that does not have the equipment to perform both jobs simultaneously.

The first four papers in Section I are general statements on child welfare, each of which was presented on a different continent but no one of which is limited in its significance by place or time. "The Challenge of the Next Decade," read in Cleveland, outlines the essential components of child welfare services, of which a financial assistance program is described as basic. "Child Welfare in Industrialized Countries," presented in Stockholm, describes the worldwide trend toward urbanization, the benefits it offers and the problems it poses for the family, the services required to assist the family to thrive under urban conditions, and the responsibility of organized child welfare as children's advocate. In "A National Child Welfare Policy," given in Melbourne, Mr. Reid discusses both the reasons the United States lacks a coherent policy and the ingredients of such a policy. "Safeguarding the Family," delivered in Pretoria, reiterates the essentiality of an economic floor, discusses the kinds of program that support the family under pressure, and contains the message, "No family is safe, no child is safe, while another family, another child remains unguarded."

Section II contains three papers that concern the relationship of public and voluntary agencies to each other. "The Role of Public and Private Agencies in Providing Services to Children" discusses the different characteristics of public and voluntary agencies, the need each has for the other, and the importance to both of citizen involvement. "Some Observations on Private Casework Agencies and Social Policy" emphasizes the responsibility of voluntary agencies to be active in effecting social policy change and staffs' need for additional knowledge if they are to carry out this responsibility. "The Role of the Private Sector in Securing the Rights of Children" speaks to the interdependence of public and private agencies, with the latter serving as advocates for children's rights and lobbyists for governmental action. In this paper Mr. Reid seriously questions the proprietary agency as a vehicle for ensuring children's rights, as he does much more forcefully in one of his published papers, "The Role of the Voluntary Sector."

Section III is composed of three papers dealing with specific child welfare services—institutional care, adoption and day care—and one discussing likenesses and differences between family and children's agencies. Although "The Role of the Modern Children's Institution" was written over 20 years ago, it is a succinct statement of sound policy that the field is still trying to implement today. "New Knowledge and New Trends in Adoption," of about the same date, stresses the need, which has been met only in part, for a much greater infusion of public and voluntary funds, as well as streamlining of agency practices, if adoption is to be achieved for the tremendous number of potentially adoptable children in foster care. In "Universal Day Care" Mr. Reid cautions against the sacrifice of quality of care, choice on the part of the mother, and appropriateness of the care to the needs of the child, under the banner of day care for all. "The Responsibility of Family and Children's Agencies for Rehabilitation of Families" cites the common philosophy of the two types of agency—viewing the family as a whole and seeing the child in the framework of the family—but notes differences in practice and clientele.

The two papers in Section IV relate to agency staffing. "Personnel Needs" emphasizes the appropriate use of professionally trained staff and of staff without such training, and suggests ways to recruit and better use trained staff. In "Educational Experience and Practice Demands," Mr. Reid urges strengthening the master's curriculum so that graduates will emerge with a more adequate knowledge base that will permit them to function at a level significantly different from that of staff members without graduate training.

Mr. Reid is a strong proponent of research to expand the knowledge base of child welfare. Examples of the application of research findings abound in his papers, as do unanswered questions that need attention, and exhortations to agency boards to assess their programs. One of the developments at the League under his leadership was the establishment of a permanent Research Center. My role in this publication is, in part, an expression of my appreciation for Mr. Reid's effectiveness in creating a climate at the League conducive to research, and for his unfailing support for the activities of the research staff.

Ann W. Shyne
Formerly Director,
CWLA Research Center

I.

CHILD
WELFARE
POLICY
AND PROGRAM

THE CHALLENGE OF THE NEXT DECADE

None of us, of course, can predict what will happen in the next 10 years, but we can examine what has happened in the last 10 years and presume that at least some of these things will keep on happening.

Our concern in the child welfare field is for the disadvantaged child—the child who for some reason does not live with a family that can give him complete nurture. We know that we are in the midst of a revolution in relation to the type of child who comes to our care and the type of family with whom we deal. This revolution can be understood only in terms of the enormous shift taking place in family life in the United States.

I review here some things of which you are well aware, but which are not apparent to the public. If we are to convince the public and achieve acceptance for the public and private programs that we are concerned with, we must keep these things in mind.

The purposes for which children's institutions and organizations were organized 50 or 100 years ago are no longer valid today. It is not the American *child* that has changed; it is the American *family* that has almost completely changed.

CHANGES IN THE AMERICAN FAMILY

When I was growing up, we and the people around us had innumerable relatives in the vicinity. I don't remember a day care center in my town, but I do know that whenever my parents needed one they had cousins or aunts who were glad to act as one. I am reasonably sure there wasn't a family counseling agency, but if my

Presented at Trusteeship for Children, an Institute for Trustees and Committee Members of Child Care Agencies, sponsored by the Welfare Federation of Cleveland and Western Reserve University, February 5, 1962.

parents had had serious marital difficulties, I know of at least one or two aunts and a grandmother who would have been glad to give any counseling that was needed.

I remember that, when an uncle and an aunt were in an automobile accident, no one worried about available institutions or foster homes for their children because there were plenty of relatives who would absorb the children as a part of their own family. That was typical of our country as a whole.

Today I haven't a relative within 600 miles, and that, too, is now quite typical. The American family today lives quite apart from its relatives, its relationship to its church is changed, and it does not have the same social resources. When a family has trouble, it usually depends upon those resources that a community has made available. If it is an average family, the odds are that it will move about once every 5 years. It no longer lives for generations in the same house or in the same town or on the same farm. It is a family that is alone in a sense that families were never alone before.

Unless we see our families in the context of a modern industrial nation that requires its families to be small and mobile, and having only limited resources of their own, we are not likely to recognize the necessity for financing, out of tax funds or Community Chest dollars, the level of social services that this particular generation of Americans needs.

EFFECTS ON CHILDREN

With these changes have come many social disadvantages to children. Children are being subjected to the hazards of a changing culture and society. Communities have not provided the resources that enable a family to remain together and to be stable. Whether it is the Deep South, where the level of services is obviously extremely poor, or one of the nation's richest states, such as Ohio, where the needs are not so obviously great, it can be easily established that we are treating thousands of our children in a way that is utterly foolish. The bill we will be paying for them later as adults will be far higher than today's costs.

As a nation, we have not faced up to the fact that our programs for children cannot be seen as charities, depending upon particularistic concerns for our fellow men, and with freedom to choose whether or not to offer help. America's heritage of private philanthropy has prevented the public from realizing that these programs are neither options nor luxuries. Having sound child welfare programs is as essential to the community as a clean water supply.

Too frequently when we speak about the number of children in a local community who are in foster homes, or on ADC, we talk of a relatively small number. We may even speak of a quarter of a million children in institutions or foster homes in our country, but the more meaningful figure is the 2½ million within this generation of children who sometime during their childhood are going to live for a protracted period outside their own homes. And when we consider that the public assistance program now includes almost 3 million children in the country, we have to extrapolate that there are going to be around 9 million children of this generation who will find themselves in a family receiving public assistance at some point in their childhood.

In other words, a very sizable proportion of our entire child population is affected. The quality of the care that we provide will determine the type of adults we rear. A survey of adults in state penitentiaries would show that roughly half had lived as children for an extended period in some form of foster care. A sizable percentage would have lived for some part of their lives in a public assistance family. We know that the emotional security and sense of self-worth such a child receives during an extremely vulnerable period of his life have a great deal to do with the type of adult he becomes.

INADEQUACY OF PUBLIC ASSISTANCE

We are talking, therefore, about a large and extremely serious problem. For example: In this city (Cleveland) children are receiving 70% of minimal budget needs. Statistics are cold and rather meaningless. This is a figure that glides over the tongue and slides through the mind rather easily. There isn't a person in this room or in this city who would willingly see a particular child in a particular family starve; yet there are obviously several million people in this state willing to see several hundred thousand children in the state starve, because somehow we have not been able to translate to the public the actual meaning of this figure.

The ADC program is the basic child welfare program in the United States. There is no private child welfare agency that can operate unless a high level of public assistance is available. Ohio, like every other state, goes through an elaborate procedure to establish the minimum amount of food, clothing and housing that a family needs. Economists in Ohio's universities, as well as other experts, spend a good deal of time finding out what a child needs in order to survive. The family that is wholly dependent upon public assistance is then arbitrarily given 70% of that figure!

Without examining the case record of a single child, we can be certain that there are a great many children under the care of public child care agencies who are there for one reason only—economic want—where the child is in foster care not because of marital breakdown per se, not because of death, but for no other reason than the erosion of a family because of having to live on a level on which it is impossible to live.

If this family has some courage, some strength, then that parent will cheat or find some way to get enough money to put food in his child's mouth or to dress him decently when he goes to school so that it is not obvious that he is on public relief. Anyone with sensitivity would do the same if his community viewed his children stigmatically.

The specialized needs of children can be met if only there is a basically decent undergirding of public assistance in the community. I want to make a few guesses, based upon current trends, of what it is board members are going to be up against in attempting to plan and make policy intelligently for our public and private child welfare agencies.

CHANGES IN INSTITUTIONS AND FOSTER HOMES

Because of medical advances over the last 30 or 40 years, death of parents has been eliminated as the basic cause of children's need of foster care. Approximately 97% of all children in foster care today have parents. Care of orphans is no longer a basic problem.

Caring for normal children who simply need good food, good shelter and good clothing is a job that no longer has to be done in the community. Therefore, agencies that are attempting to gear institutional programs to care for normal children on a 24-hour basis have no business being in existence, and the United Fund has no business financing them.

I think that there is a relatively clear trend that will make institutions or forms of group care for children unlike anything we know at present. There is a growing need for institutions for the treatment of disturbed children. These institutions have extremely high costs. To the extent that that treatment proves successful and produces results, there will be greater acceptance of the high costs.

In the next 10 or 20 years we are going to see a gradual diminishing of foster homes. One of the reasons for this is urbanization—increasing apartment living and small houses where people simply do not have room to care for extra children. Another reason is that among the middle class it is not so acceptable to care for a foster child as it once was.

The tremendous mobility of the American family is also having a serious effect on the stability of foster homes. In a recent national study, the League found that well over 25% of all children in foster home care had been moved at least four times during their period of care. The fact that over one-fourth of all American families move each year has something to do with that statistic.

We are going to have to change the nature of foster home care, particularly in coping with the growing problem of the minority-group child in foster care. The trustees of children's agencies in the great northern cities have a double problem. Increasingly, their programs must care for these children. We all have prejudices, regardless of how free of them we think we are. The limits to which boards go to rationalize why it is they are not taking care of a proportionate share of nonwhite children is interesting to see in the North. In the South, the situation is at least simple and clear. Unquestionably some of the problems of housing and of neighborhoods accentuate the problems with respect to foster care. I believe that we must experiment with subsidizing some homes, or paying higher boarding home rates, or employing foster parents as full-time employees of agencies. We must also set aside a portion of all of our public housing—not just lower income housing projects, but some of our middle income housing—to be used exclusively for families employed by agencies, in order to obtain decent foster home care for many nonwhite children who need this care.

ROLE OF DAY CARE AND HOMEMAKER SERVICE

There will be an increasing necessity for good programs of day care. Fortunately, at the moment, there is some federal recognition of this fact. Since World War II there has been an ever-rising percentage of mothers of young children working in industry. We must have some social provision—not on the philosophical basis of a social basket for the poor—for day care as a public utility, recognizing that one cannot have millions of mothers going into industry without making some provision for their children. I think we will be changing some of our ideas as to the type of day care that has to be provided, in terms of several types of care geared to the needs of different children and different families. Another area of need is the use of homemakers, which must unquestionably be increased, both in the medical and social welfare fields.

To me it is obvious that we will have to ask agencies that are no longer meeting today's needs either to change or go out of existence and let somebody else spend the community dollar. If we don't, there will be many children whose needs are not met.

NEED FOR RESEARCH

Each of us on an agency board faces two facts: first, that funds are not keeping up with the number of children in need; and second, that there are limits to the amount of tax money that can be spent, or the amount of money that can be raised through private philanthropy. We must make sure that the dollar that is available is being wisely utilized. We spend an extremely small portion of our child welfare dollar for research to find out whether we are doing what we think we are doing. Research will undoubtedly challenge many of the concepts we now have, many that we as professionals believe are right. Research must go forward, however, and every community has a responsibility to engage in it.

In the last 10 years there have been radical changes in adoption practice. Many of the changes were due to the application of research findings. For example, the average age at which a baby is placed for adoption today is less than one half of what it was 10 years ago. Today, anyone would defend the premise that children should be placed for adoption at an average age of less than 3 months. Ten years ago 9 months was not uncommon, and 6 months was a conservative average. The changes that have taken place in this field have increased the value the community is getting for its dollar, and the value all of us are getting from seeing that the needs of children and those who adopt them are being met.

At the Child Welfare League of America we believe that research funds should be spent first in those areas where we are most certain of our standards. Children are fairly safe as long as professionals disagree about what is best for them. It's when they *agree* that one has a responsibility to make sure that the course agreed upon will produce the best results.

Much more has to be done locally to finance a basic examination of results. Most of the current funds for research are from national private foundations or the federal government. To do more locally in this area of research, agency boards must feel convinced about the need to assess what they do. When you are on a board for 3 years, 5 years, 20 years, you get to thinking about an agency as yours. If a study suggests that what you are doing is not very good or that the results you are getting do not justify the money you are spending, it hits not only at the professionals who are caring for the children, but at board members too. The willingness to examine what one is doing is the heart of every change.

CHANGE IN AGENCY SERVICE PATTERNS

Another major change we will encounter in the next 10 years is in the pattern of our social agencies. Take, for example, the pattern of services for unmarried mothers. In most communities an unmarried mother has to run around to a half-dozen agencies to get service. Rarely is there just one agency in the community that will give a total service—providing counseling if that is what she needs, providing foster home care or adoption if that is what she needs, providing the financial assistance that she will certainly need for medical care.

The number of cities in which the community chest policy will not permit its agencies to spend money on the out-of-town unmarried mother is amazing—this despite the fact that the nature of her problem causes her to travel to gain anonymity. Cleveland's unmarried mothers go to Cincinnati or New York. New York's go to Cleveland. Chest restrictions based on residence must be eliminated.

Much stronger public protective services will also have to be developed. A single service should be available so that, when a family is obviously mistreating its children, there is one place to which the community can turn and make certain that the agency investigates and offers help, and if necessary takes police action. My view is that this by its very nature has to be a public service, and cannot be financed by private funds.

We must think of programs that will assist us in early identification and prevention of the problems of children and their families, instead of attempting to cure the disturbed child or help the broken family *after* the damage has been done. Unless we prevent problems, we have no chance of holding the line on the number of children and families needing services and on the tax and private dollars to pay for these services. A basic problem is how to get money for preventive programs.

PUBLIC UNDERSTANDING AND SUPPORT

People pay for things they understand. The fact that it costs a given number of dollars a day to care for a child with polio does not bother us because we understand the necessity. Yet the child with a crippled mind instead of a crippled leg has a need that we somehow don't understand and therefore do not pay for.

Translating the need into terms that people understand is primarily a job of identifying what is actually going on in the community. I am not going to suggest ways in which this can be done. But I suspect there is some reticence on the part of the administrative agencies caring for children to make crystal clear—in terms of individual families and individual case situations—just what it is they are administering and the very low level of care they are providing. I suspect, also, that many private agencies worry when there is too much talk about the effects of low standards, because they are afraid it will undermine the support they are already getting. Yet I submit that unless the poor quality and the poor standards that we manage to achieve are made clear to the public, we have no chance of getting an adequate level of support. In some studies of foster care made by my own organization, we have created a fair amount of misunderstanding—part of it is inevitable, part of it could have been avoided—by talking about what we found: that at least half the children in foster care in the United States do not belong there, that many of them could have been placed for adoption had there been decent programs available, or returned to their own homes. In a certain sense we are saying that we are doing a bad job, yet we must make these things absolutely clear in terms that people understand. We must show them the effect of neglect, of substandard community financing, of lack of professionally trained personnel, of high caseloads, on the lives of children. Unless we do there is no chance of getting the financing we need.

Many of us believe we are taxed as far as we can go and that we are giving as much as we can to the Community Chest or United Fund—that at some point there is a limit. The only way we can understand that we are not at that limit is to see the level on which we are forcing other families to live.

I know of one community where the churches held a series of dinners, the menu consisting of food that could be purchased with the money that was available to relief families in that community. As a result, the people in that community began to understand what it meant to have 70% of the amount of money that one needs to survive. There are ways of illustrating and dramatizing the plight of these families to counteract the common misunderstanding and criticism of public assistance recipients.

PURCHASE OF SERVICE

I suggest that, if the community does agree on a policy to purchase services from private child care agencies, thought be given to the philosophy and principles on purchase of care that will achieve the soundest development of both private and public agencies. I believe that some purchase of care is valuable and necessary in a community; but unwise purchase of care can lead to the morass that exists in so many communites without a rational pattern of financing private agencies by public sources.

One consideration is that the public dollar used to purchase care should not replace the private dollar. Rather, public money should be used to enrich and improve the standards of the private agencies receiving it. In spite of the fact that Cleveland has a good record of community fund giving, giving has not kept up with population, nor has it kept up with the need for financing expensive specialized services. This is true throughout the country. Also true, unfortunately, in most parts of the country is the growing disparity between the amount of money going into health services and group work services, and the amount going into the casework field. United Fund financing for casework services has not kept up with the financing of other areas. This disparity should not be allowed to continue, if it can be prevented, and it certainly should not be encouraged by simply passing off to the tax dollar the responsibilities that are now being carried by private contributions. It is extremely important that we keep alive the concept of personal responsibility for one's fellowmen. Private agencies and private giving are necessary for the moral health of a community.

There has been a tendency, when public funds are used to purchase private care, for Community Chest budget committees to say: "That type of financing is no longer our responsibility; let the public agencies do the whole job." One way to solve this problem is to establish a ratio of private and public dollars for the private agency. For example, most people agree that the predominant source of financing of private agencies should be private funds. Therefore, a policy limiting the amount of care to be purchased from any one private agency to no more than 50% of its budget would make sense to me. Now, to many people this may seem a high ratio. They might well say that this is too much public money to be going into a private agency's budget. There are parts of the United States, however, in which as much as 99% of so-called private agencies' budgets is coming from public funds. This is a very unhealthy situation. If we believe in maintaining a balance between private enterprise, private philanthropy and governmental financing, we need a yardstick that provides a definition of what *is* a private agency.

Another question that has to be decided is: What should be the basis of the public agency's payments to the private agency? I believe that the only sound basis is a cost accounting of the private agency's service. Reimbursement should be based on 100% of that cost. Flat rates that apply to all agencies, or rates that apply only to certain elements of the private agency's costs, such as service costs or administration costs, should be avoided.

The public agency must have the final decision as to when it purchases care and what it agrees to buy. The public agency should not buy care from agencies whose standards are low. It should insist upon low caseloads, properly qualified personnel, etc. It is possible to work out quality improvement devices that build into the purchase of care system. This concept that the public agency must take final responsibility for the care it purchases is a very important one. We must not distort the balance of relationships between public and private agencies by permitting the private agency to determine what type of care the child needs. This caution is not farfetched. For example, there are several states and communities in the United States where, by law, a public agency may give care to a child only when it can attest in writing that there is no private agency that will take the child. What usually follows is that the public agency must pay for that care, even though the care is substandard. If a child needs foster home care, for example, and a private agency with a 1000-bed institution wants to place the child in an institution, the public agency paying for the care has no right under such laws to insist that the child get the type of care needed.

Everyone in this conference room, whether wearing the hat of a board member of a private agency or a public agency, is in essence a representative of both. Unless the board members of private agencies are as much concerned about the child in public care as they are about the child in the care of their own agency, unless they are as much concerned about the level of public financing as about that of private financing, the children of the community inevitably will not receive good care. The board members of child welfare agencies are the only people in the community who know the real needs of the community's children. I wish that the public agencies made better use of citizen advisory boards; such use should be encouraged.

If all of you really regard yourselves as stewards not of a single child care agency but of every child in the community who needs attention and care, then the next 10 years can only be years of progress.

CHILD WELFARE
IN INDUSTRIALIZED
COUNTRIES

Child welfare services are the institutionalized way by which society ensures that children will have the care, protection and treatment they need when their parents, for any of a variety of reasons, are not able to provide these essentials. Said another way, child welfare services are alternative ways that have evolved to nurture, care and protect children, to foster their optimum development and social functioning, and, when necessary, to remedy or ameliorate their problems. The extent to which child welfare services are needed does, and should, vary widely with individual families. For example, in some families all that is needed is a service that *supports* or reinforces the ability of the parents to meet the child's needs. In others, the services must go further and *supplement* the care that the child receives from his parents or the services must compensate for certain inadequacies. In still others, the services must actually *substitute* for parental care.

All parents need the help of some community services to rear their children; some need more than others because of special problems in the child, limitations within themselves, or conditions in the community. It is to this latter—the community and especially the urbanized community—that I would like to draw attention. What influence do industrialized, urban communities have on parental functioning and the degree of help parents need to rear their children? The extent and character of help parents need *should* constitute a blueprint or diagram for the child welfare services a community provides. And yet, I know of no place in the world where

Presented at the World Child Welfare Congress, Stockholm, September 8, 1969. Published in International Child Welfare Review, *January 1970, pp. 75ff.*

child welfare services exist proportionate to need. Further, it is often in industrialized urbanized settings, where needs are desperate, that flagrant inadequacies of services are found. The nonexistence or deplorable inadequacies of child welfare services in industrialized areas throughout the world prevail not because the child welfare field does not care, but because the problems that confront the field are too massive for us yet to have found solutions. Perhaps if we look at the picture of urbanization, we can gain some perspective. Perhaps we can then remedy some of the conditions that to date are destroying our hopes for millions of urban children who are living under adverse conditions.

THE PACE OF URBANIZATION

First, let me quote some widely publicized statistics on urbanization. During the 100 years that saw the world population double, the urban population increased five times. Less than 200 years ago, less than 2% of the world's population lived in cities and towns. Today, one-third of the world lives in urban areas. Further, it is predicted that by the end of the century, two-thirds of an anticipated 6 billion population will live in urban areas. Today, one-third of urban dwellers, or about 12% of the world population, live in shanty towns of more than 100,000 inhabitants on the fringes of our cities. Other millions live in slums in the middle of the cities. All parts of the world are in the throes of urbanization. Here are some examples:

In Russia, the urban population has doubled in the last 30 years. More than half the population of Australia lives within seven cities. Japan's metropolitan population almost doubled between 1950 and 1969. The population of Bombay increased three times in the last 20 years, and Peking's doubled. In Africa, the population of Dar Es Salaam doubled in the last 10 years. Populations of Accra and Luanda tripled and that of Conakry increased four times in the last 5 years. Populations of Santiago and Bogota, in South America, doubled between 1940 and 1960; those of Sao Paulo, Lima and Mexico City increased three times, and that of Caracas, five times.

The western nations are not being affected so acutely by urbanization today for the simple reason that the process has been a much, much longer one. Another factor that makes for differences between the West and the East is the birth rate. The present European birth rate is 19 per 1000, as against 42 per 1000 in Asia and 46 in Africa.

I doubt that anyone who attends a world congress on child welfare can think about these dramatic rises in urbanization without experiencing some apprehension for the well-being of children. Unfortunately, I can conjure up no rationale to dispel our apprehension. I do think, however, that it is important for us to remind ourselves that industrialization and urban living do have *some* benefits for *some* children, e.g., higher standards of living, better health care, better nutrition, better education, tremendous cultural advantages, career opportunities, etc. This observation leaves us with the as-yet unanswerable question of how the benefits, rather than the hazards, of industrialization can be experienced by *all* children. It leaves us with our major concern—namely, the frequent negative effect that rapid urbanization has had on the family and the culture from which the family grew.

EFFECTS OF URBANIZATION ON THE FAMILY

In most countries, the population movement from rural areas to cities has meant that the family could no longer function as it had for past centuries. In almost every culture throughout the world, the family once had its own built-in social security system. The family then did not consist, as it does now in many urban societies, of a nuclear group of father, mother and several children. Rather, the basic family unit was an extended one that included grandparents, aunts, uncles, cousins and, in some countries, persons outside of blood ties. Under these circumstances, children were frequently not just the responsibility of the father and mother, but of a tribal group or some larger lineal system. If a parent died, his brothers or sisters or others in the "family" had an absolute responsibility to care for and rear the child. There was never a question about this responsibility and, consequently, systems of foster care as we know them were not necessary.

In addition to its responsibility for children, the extended family provided other functions that we now call social services. For example, if marital counseling were needed, there was always a grandparent or other revered elder who was glad to step in to counsel the young adults. Homemaker services or home health aides were provided by relatives. Provision of day care was obviously not necessary when there were many female relatives who assumed partial responsibility for the child. Thus, the whole elaborate structure of child welfare services that is needed in an urban society was unnecessary, or at least, far less necessary, in a rural and nonindustrialized environment.

The family that moves from a small town or rural area to an urban community is subject to severe strains, regardless of the nation in which this move occurs. In some areas of the world, however, the transition is beyond the comprehension of most of us. Try to imagine what happens when a family that has lived in a culture unchanged for centuries moves, in a period of a few days, to a 20th century industrialized metropolis. For some such parents, the transition is impossible; they strive to cling to their old ways, their old culture and mores. For the children, however, change—though fraught with uncertainty—is inevitable. Often it is the child who must serve for his parents as a bridge from the old culture to the new. In the process, severe tensions can grow. The child is likely to regard his parents as having lost guardian and mentor status, as being old-fashioned, unknowing, unsophisticated. He may discard their values long before he has had a chance to internalize any of his own from his "new world." Rootless, without values of his own, without the counsel and support of his elders, he is likely to drift into delinquency. Even if his behavior is not delinquent in the eyes of his new culture, it may be delinquent in the eyes of his parents, with the result that the emotional losses and frictions are compounded.

Another tragic condition is created when the move into the city forces the role of the father and the mother to be reversed. This shift often occurs when economic pressures require that all able-bodied members of the family get employment in order for the family to even survive in the city. Frequently jobs are more available to women than they are to men. The mother or daughters may become the breadwinners, while the fathers and sons, unable to find employment, become dejected homemakers. For the father, the shift from the traditional role of provider, protector and controller of the female members of his family can be deeply upsetting. This shift can, in fact, severely threaten the internal dynamics of family life. For the mother, the new role of being the provider may be equally unsatisfactory. The unfamiliar and frightening aspects of having to leave the shelter of home each day may far outweigh the advantages. But whether the parental roles are changed or remain traditional, loss of the familiar and fears of the unknown generally decrease the family's ability to function as a family.

Another severe strain results when, particularly for the older adolescent or youth, the city may not have occupations to absorb his labor. In the rural area from which he came, his labor would have been used in agricultural pursuits or homecrafts, for example. The phenomenon of hordes of young people without jobs is common to a great many large cities and urban areas, and in itself creates another severe problem.

The pressures of urban life, whether on the newcomer family or on the family that has resided in the large city for several generations, are obviously very severe. The combination of incessant pressures of urban life, a repeated sense of failure, and inability to cope with multiple problems adversely affects the quality of parenting. Frequently too, the accumulated pressures precipitate or contribute to high incidence of mental illness in metropolitan populations. The mental illness of parents, of course, has a severe impact on the whole family and particularly on children. Perplexed and bereft by the mysterious changes in the parents, children react adversely. When hospitalization of a parent is necessary, the potential benefits are frequently minimized or treatment is even terminated prematurely because of overcrowding in hospitals. The effects upon the already disadvantaged child are intensified. This painful cycle needs no further elaboration.

One of the most serious problems that characterize urban life in all too many countries, except perhaps such fortunate countries as Sweden and Denmark, is a severe shortage of decent housing. Disintegration of the central core of large cities is common to many countries. The growth of slums and the intense concentrations of people in small areas are not phenomena peculiar to Hong Kong, Manila, Tokyo or New York; they are found in hundreds of large cities. Worst of all are the shanty towns, barrios or favelas that mushroom around many of our cities. These conditions are particularly bad in South America, Asia and Africa, where millions of families are living in makeshift housing—"homes" built out of paper or scrap metal, without light, water or sanitation, where 10 or 15 persons may live in a single room. But they exist elsewhere—from Paris to Rio de Janeiro. In Paris, for instance, one can see the makeshift shacks built by the Portuguese and Spanish and other groups attracted from countries in which opportunities for decent wages and employment are low. These slums, of course, are the breeding grounds for the gravest problems of children—premature births, birth defects, infant mortality, extreme malnutrition, and chronically poor health.

When families that have lived for perhaps 20 generations in a highly regulated set of family relationships are forced to adjust to an alien culture that is devoid of sustaining qualities, family disorganization is common. How could it be otherwise under the tremendous impact of even the few conditions I have mentioned?

SOCIETAL SUPPORTS FOR THE URBAN FAMILY

In essence, the family has lost many of its built-in social protections and social services in the process of becoming urbanized. If society could subscribe to this thesis, its approach would be that it is not a family's fault that it requires child welfare services or other social services. We should accept the fact that the pressures of today's urbanized society impede the family's ability to provide for itself. It therefore becomes incumbent upon society to help provide for it. In other words, provision of services should not be made on the basis that people who need them are exceptional or that personal fault, pathology or weakness causes the family to need them. Rather, it is a natural need and one for which society must make provision, not out of a sense of charity or philanthropy, but because welfare services are essential to the well-being of society as a whole, just as clean water, sanitation and public transportation are essential to the general well-being. Child welfare services should be available to all children and all families, because any family in time may come to need them. Many persons refer to this concept of universal availability as the social utility concept.

Unfortunately, social work, particularly that taught in the United States, has until recently conceived most situations requiring child welfare services as evidence of individual or family pathology. We too frequently have looked to see what was exceptional or—to put it more bluntly—what was "wrong" about the family that needed child welfare services. Speaking for practice in the United States, I can say that we have veered too far on the side of looking at and for pathology. We have underplayed alignment with health—that is to say, with the healthy aspects of children and families. This, and our one-to-one treatment approach, have resulted in our serving only a miniscule fraction of those who need help. Varying eligibility requirements have in fact been purposely established to limit the numbers who can get help. For whatever reasons, in every industrialized area in the world this is common: children are in want, they are unprotected from physical and emotional hazards, but it is to only a few that help is given.

The social utility concept aims to change this picture. It proposes that social services be viewed as a right. Further, it takes for granted, just as there is nothing exceptional about a family that needs a public school system in order to educate its child, there is nothing exceptional about a family that needs public day care, homemaker service, or even, on occasion, foster care for its children. As our goal, we must work for universal availability of child welfare services.

SERVICES TO SUPPORT PARENTAL FUNCTIONING

I have no doubt that our first line of defense in behalf of children must be services that support or reinforce the ability of parents to meet the child's needs. There should be a major development of programs designed to assist parents with parenting. Implicit in this approach, of course, is helping harassed urban parents experience being accepted for what they are or would like to be; helping them develop confidence in themselves; helping them understand what is usually expected of a parent and what is required to meet children's needs; helping them discover how they can use help, especially if they have never had it before; helping them establish connections within the community. Such services might take forms such as having direct contact with the child, counseling with parents about their anxieties, teaching a mother how to market, or establishing social centers or parents' clubs devoted to parenting craft and homemaking.

No service such as these, however, can substitute for enough money to buy adequate food, shelter and clothing and to permit participation in community life. It is essential to minimize environmental stress and prevent or modify conditions that contribute to deprivation before, or at the same time as, attempting to help a child or parent change.

Because most countries have allocated such limited resources to enhance family functioning, many parents in large urban areas receive no help. Frustration and desperation sometimes take their toll in the form of child abuse and neglect. The abhorrent facts cause some responsible observers in the United States to view child abuse as one of the greatest causes of child death. Seeing to it that no child is abused or neglected is the community's business. The very hugeness of cities, their anonymity, and their occupants' intense preoccupation with their own survival nonetheless make it difficult for the community to demonstrate that it cares.

HOMEMAKER AND DAY CARE SERVICE

Next in order of priority are services designed to supplement parental care or to compensate for certain inadequacies in such care. I have in mind homemaker service and day care service. The former has existed without formal structure for centuries. Urbanization, with its distances, its complex transportation networks and its isolation of families, has interrupted the spontaneous homemaking help traditionally provided by neighbors and relatives in times of illness or stress. An urban family today, though surrounded by hundreds of thousands of people, may know no one on whom it can call. Therefore, again something that was once taken care of naturally by the extended family now must be provided by society itself. A homemaker service program, such as that in France, can go far beyond that of a housekeeper or substitute caretaker for children. Frequently, a skilled homemaker can help an ill or fearful mother by teaching her better methods of housekeeping, purchasing or child care. By her example and training, the homemaker can bring added stability to a family. The benefits of her help thus last far beyond the temporary period of crisis.

Day care, as a supplement to parental care, holds tremendous potential for thousands of city children who acutely need it. It is in this area that we in the U.S. anticipate the greatest development of child welfare services in the next 10 years. The Head Start program in the United States, which had its predecessors in many other countries, is one example of day care. Experience in Israel, Russia, Yugoslavia and other countries indicated earlier that one way to overcome the enormous cultural gap between the poor rural family and the industrialized civilization in which it moved was through programs that supplement and enrich education by the use of day care facilities.

For many urban parents who have limited education and grossly inadequate wages, the stresses and strains of urban life are overwhelming, and they are not able to give their very young children the stimulation and the education they need. Through an enriched program of early childhood education and child development, day care offers an opportunity to improve the standards of the whole community. The work of Piaget and others has been a stimulus for development of better early childhood education throughout the world.

Day care services should be organized in a way that makes them readily available to every neighborhood. Their hours must be geared to the needs of the child and the mother and not to the needs of the workers in the day care centers. A day care center must not be thought of simply as a place for babysitting or for child watching, but rather as a center in which health, educational, social and many other services of benefit to the family can be located.

In some countries, including the United States, there has been some development of supervised family day care homes. These are homes in which a woman agrees to accept from two to five children for care in her own home during the day. The homes are supervised by social agencies. Frequently the day care mother is provided with recreational assistance and equipment. The home is certified by the state, and a mother seeking day care for her child has assurance that decent care will be provided.

Regardless of whether the day care is in a home or a center, the service should be viewed as a basic social utility. Nowhere is this view more appropriate than in industrialized areas.

FOSTER CARE AND ADOPTION

Next, I speak briefly of services designed to substitute for parental care either partly or wholly, according to the child's individual needs—foster care, both institutional and foster family care, and adoption. Family breakdown, increased by the tensions of urban life, makes foster care a vital service. However, at a time when the need for foster homes has expanded because of increasing family disintegration, the supply of foster homes has generally decreased. In the United States this decrease has been created by several factors: 1) as housing units have become smaller, individual families do not have room for foster children; 2) after the children grow up, families tend to move into smaller living quarters, where again there is no space for foster children; 3) the increasing employment of women in industry means that fewer are available to serve as foster mothers. These trends have necessitated experimenting with forms of foster care different from the old system of paying foster parents an amount approximately equal to out-of-pocket expense, but including no payment for the foster parents' services. In the United States we are now developing some experiments whereby foster parents either are employees of the agency and are paid a decent living wage, or else the payment to the foster parents includes a significant service fee. Caring for foster children should be seen as a desirable and socially accepted way of earning a living—and it will be, if the service fees are high enough.

Another development that has come in part out of the shortage of foster homes has been the creation of what we in the U.S. call group homes. These are ordinary houses or apartments that are rented or purchased by social agencies as a residence for a group of children and paid foster parents. England and other countries have developed this concept rather widely.

The shortage of family-type facilities in densely populated areas has had one good effect on foster care. It has forced the child welfare field to take a second and more benign look at institutional care. The results of the reassessment are encouraging in that many institutions throughout the world are revitalizing their services. Some are becoming part of a network of community services in order that joint effort will yield comprehensive coverage as well as selectivity of the resource most appropriate to a given child's needs at a given time.

For some children, complete and permanent care by persons other than their biological parents is essential. The permanent planning may or may not be necessitated by the marital status of the child's parents. Regardless of whether the family is a one-parent or two-parent family, or whether the couple are married, the parent or parents should have access to a variety of services that will enable them to plan most effectively in the child's interest. As important as adoption service is, however, it is appropriate to only a relatively small number of dependent and neglected children.

YOUTH PROGRAMS

In addition to the various services that have been mentioned for young children and parents, there is great need for organized youth activities. Urban areas and villages have over the centuries developed natural ways in which youths could congregate and socialize. Today, welfare services for youths require the best of our imagination. Too frequently in the urban areas true neighborhoods do not exist. As a consequence, adolescents and youths often frequent undesirable places—pool halls, beer taverns—or they aimlessly wander the streets. Child welfare agencies should organize youth services that meet the adolescents' need to congregate in small groups—a place where the atomosphere is healthy and where supervision exists essentially to keep order and to provide some guidance on request. Such youth centers vary from simple neighborhood "hangouts" to youth centers with rather elaborate programs.

The Russians, Israelis and others have developed excellent examples of highly organized youth programs that seek to increase their adolescents' knowledge and understanding of the world around them and develop interest and motivation. These include group trips to historical and archeological sites, and various other cultural and educational activities. Mountain climbing, camping, canoe and boat trips and other forms of vacation resources are essential parts of such programs.

THE CHILD WELFARE AGENCY AS ADVOCATE FOR CHILDREN

I have spoken directly and indirectly of the complexities of urban life, of the stresses they bring to families, and of the urgent need to establish and extend services that can enhance a gratifying way of life for children and their families. Where does the child welfare field fit into this picture? Alone, it is relatively helpless in overcoming some of the basic problems of uuban life. Housing, transportation, inadequate earnings, lack of job opportunities, lack of educational resources and of health care—all of these are outside the ken of child welfare. But it is here that the child welfare field must play a major role—that of advocacy. The child welfare worker is sometimes in the best position to relay the horrible impact of poor urban conditions on the lives of children. By making these conditions graphic, by bringing them to the attention of the general public, legislators and others able to effect change, child welfare workers can perform a very important function in addition to their technical services.

Many people are simply unaware of the devastating effect of urban life on children; they do not realize how important intervention is to improve children's lives. Many other people lack understanding of the need for services. Still others harbor prejudices and ill will toward those who need help. They illogically subscribe to the thesis that services "pamper" and perpetuate dependency, illegitimacy, and so on. Public education is essential to overcome such prejudices and ignorance. Responsibility for providing public education belongs to those who see distress firsthand—that is, to child welfare executives, boards of directors, and agency personnel. A primary responsibility of all child welfare agencies is to propagandize for the development of services for children. We in the field should seek no choice other than that of being advocates for children. Child welfare cannot remain subordinated. Current world events alone are ample evidence of what children as "tomorrow's leaders" require today. Child welfare agencies must also take responsibility for helping to interpret to the general public the impact of the social consequences of urbanization; many city dwellers who have lived there for generations do not realize the impact of the city on newcomers.

In closing, I point out that it was nearly 50 years ago (1923) that the International Union for Child Welfare first proclaimed that "the child must be brought up in the consciousness that his talents must be devoted to the service of his fellowman." Our progress toward this goal has fallen short of the hopes of each of us; we have provided few of the world's needy children with what it takes to let them have concern for another. I reiterate, therefore, that only if we become chief advocates for children can we anticipate their healthy development. Only then can we anticipate a lessening of the human distress that now exists under urbanized conditions.

A NATIONAL
CHILD WELFARE POLICY

The subject that the conference has been asked to consider today is, "A National Policy on Child Welfare." Before accepting your invitation to come to Australia and address this subject in particular, I thought hard about why I had been invited. After all, I do not come from a country that can be said to have "a national policy on child welfare." Although the United States may be considered the richest country in the world, with the highest standard of living, it cannot be said to have one of the most enlightened policies, or, in fact, any national policy toward children.

Then, I thought of my association with the International Union for Child Welfare and of the opportunities that it has given me to learn and study the child welfare programs of many countries. However, that association alone could not account for the invitation because there are many people far more knowledgeable than I about the international scene, and better qualified to discuss the subject.

In fact, it was sometime after I had accepted the invitation (because I wanted to return to Australia and learn more about your child welfare programs) that I realized the logic in asking an American to join in your deliberations. Our countries in part share a common heritage. Both of us originally were English colonies, inevitably sharing a common heritage of English common laws, attitudes toward poverty, toward work, toward the disadvantaged. The English poor laws, indentured servitude and sweet charity are common in the memories of both our countries.

Both countries were first populated in part by the dejected and the rejected, by the convicted and the condemned, by the poor and those who no longer had a place in their native land. Both soon attracted people of the same sort from scores of other countries. Both

---

Presented at the Australian Child Care Conference, Melbourne, February 1972.

nations went on to conquer a wilderness, to develop an extremely strong sense of individual worth, of independence, of rugged individualism, of the spirit of pioneer helpfulness—of joining together in a sense of neighborliness and kinship—and at the same time a sense of "every man for himself and the devil take the hindmost."

We are both democracies with somewhat similar forms of government. We both have states, and now we both have dollars and cents. We both have a history of racial bigotry. We both have been less than humane to the original occupants of our lands when we found them—the Aborigine in Australia, the American Indian in the United States.

I am sure I have carried this similarity far enough. If I am not careful, someone will rise up in the audience and say, "But we're not that much like the Yanks."

In talking about "a national policy on child welfare," I will not be able to talk about a national child welfare policy for Australia, for I know too little about Australia. In reading about your programs, I am sure I have not always understood them. So, if I make assumptions that are incorrect or draw conclusions that are false, I hope you will forgive me. Instead, the Conference Committee has graciously permitted me to draw heavily upon my experience with the Child Welfare League of America in the United States. Perhaps some of that experience will be germane to Australia because of our similarities. Some will not, of course.

I first want to examine why a coherent national policy of child welfare does not exist in the United States. This negative approach may assist us later in examining what are the necessary components of a child welfare policy. And finally, we shall examine what can be done to bring about a unified policy.

WHY NO COHERENT CHILD WELFARE POLICY IN THE UNITED STATES

I said earlier that the United States does not have a coherent child welfare policy. I suspect that Australia is one of the nations that also lacks a clear one. Some nations, however, do, in terms of the importance they place on child life and on assisting the family in the rearing of the child. Soviet Russia and Israel are outstanding examples. They have a relatively clear conviction about children being their future, and they follow that conviction by investing in the nurture of their children to a far greater degree than do many western nations.

In the United States our policies are a hodgepodge. We have some excellent things and some that are very poor. There are confusion and ambivalence about children or, at least, about the children of the poor. Children in general do not have a high priority as compared with adults. Children's services lag behind those that exist for adults.

Attitude Toward Rights of Children

The rights of children are not clearly spelled out in our laws, and in many areas children seem to have no rights. The care and protection a child will receive vary widely in the United States, depending upon where he or she lives. One state may spend 20 times more per capita for child welfare services than another. One state will have poor services and another of equal wealth, excellent services.

One of the basic reasons for these lacks and disparities is our English heritage in its attitude toward poverty, the deification of work, and the granting to parents of absolute responsibility for and power over their children.

A basic concept in a civilized society is that those who are helpless need a measure of protection. Domestic animals are relatively helpless. So concerned people developed societies for the prevention of cruelty to animals. Until the last part of the 19th century, there were no laws that prohibited the abuse of children in the United States. The first case of child abuse brought before the courts was prosecuted under animal abuse laws. Although we have protective services for animals throughout the country today, only a few of our major cities have effective protective services for children. Contributions to the Society for the Prevention of Cruelty to Animals run many times higher than contributions to the Society for the Prevention of Cruelty to Children.

The heart of the matter is that people are willing to pay taxes or make contributions to protect animals, but are not willing to do so for children. Why? Has it to do with the way we regard children as the property of their parents rather than as independent human beings with their own rights? I think part of the answer is found here. Let me give a few illustrations.

It was not too many years ago that parents had absolute rights over their children, including the right in Roman times to kill them as punishment. Children were once valuable chattels. Their labor was worth more than the cost of feeding them. English common laws were zealous in protecting the rights of property, including the property that was a child. Until 1930 there was still one state in the United States that permitted children to be passed from one hand to another, primarily for adoption, using a deed that was exactly the same legal instrument used to pass a piece of property from one hand to another.

Courts in the United States have been very zealous in protecting the rights of parents, to the point that children are badly damaged. If a child is placed in a foster home or institution by his parents and they cease to support him financially and practically abandon him, it is nonetheless extremely difficult to get a court to sever parental rights and allow the child to be placed in an adoptive home. In one state, the courts have ruled that if there is any evidence that the parents have shown any interest in their child, such as sending the child a postcard once a year, this is proof that they have not abandoned the child. The courts are far more zealous in guarding the rights of the parents than the interests of the child.

Attitude Toward the Poor

Discrimination against children can also be found in laws governing the administration of financial assistance to dependent persons. In many ways, attitudes among large sectors of the American public toward the poor who must seek public assistance are not very different from those of the era of the Elizabethan poor laws. Most people are inclined to believe that those seeking public assistance are shiftless, lazy, dishonest, oversexed and alcoholic. They find it difficult to accept the fact that people seek public assistance because of unemployment, illness, lack of education that disqualifies them from modern jobs, the disappearance of the need for common labor, sharp economic disruptions, etc.

Those making the laws and administering the public assistance programs are, therefore, so intent on trying to prevent cheating, fraud, and persons' staying on public assistance for any longer than necessary that they set up rules and regulations that inevitably badly damage children. For example, if a deserted mother with three children is receiving public assistance and she refuses to accept a job, her share of the family's allowance may be taken away. Obviously, the mother still has to eat; the whole family will have to eat less.

An aged couple receiving public assistance gets as much as a mother and three children. The aged do need help and, of course, they also vote. The children suffer because of the negative attitudes toward the dependent parents. Also, children do not vote. In the State of Texas, the allowance for a "seeing eye" dog is greater than that for an adolescent boy.

Examples are found in other areas from which it is clear that the interests of children are subordinated to other interests. Although child labor in the cities has been almost eliminated in the United States, powerful agricultural interests have prevented passage or enforcement of child labor laws in rural areas. Those agricultural interests still have a stake in seeing to it that the children of poor farm workers and migrant workers labor in their fields.

Twelve million mothers work in the United States. Yet, there are only about 650,000 licensed places in day care centers. At least one of the reasons is that many influential men still stick to the Victorian idea that women should not work. If women do work, they are said to be working for frivolous reasons; therefore, let them take care of their own children. These same men may employ 500 women in their plants, but their awareness of present-day facts is not yet powerful enough to overcome their deeply ingrained prejudices.

A Question of Priorities

A nation's priorities can often get in the way of a sound national policy for children. In the United States there are long waiting lists for child guidance clinics. It is difficult and expensive to find an opening in a residential treatment center for emotionally disturbed children. Day care, as mentioned, is in very short supply. Almost all remedial and treatment services are overburdened. And the answer to the question, "Why is this so?", is that we cannot afford it. But we can afford a very expensive war, space shots to the moon, huge subsidies for agriculture and a multibillion-dollar highway system. It is not a question of "can't afford"; it is a question of priorities.

It can be, however, that people have not had a chance to vote on priorities and do not know what they are not getting. Children's needs often remain unobserved because there is not an effective lobby to bring them to the legislators and the general public who affect what the legislators do, whereas there are very effective lobbies for such things as highways, mining, the defense program, etc.

The illusions and fantasies that a people maintains also can cruelly handicap services for families and children. In the United States, as is obvious to anyone who views its movies, people are sentimental over the period of western expansion when rugged pioneers opened up a continent. Conquering Indians and storms, heat and drought, families built homesteads for themselves and became successful ranchers and presumably lived happily ever after. They did not need any government subsidy or help. They had little need for social services. If the mother and father were working a farm, they did not need a day care center—they took the children with them into the fields. If marital difficulties developed between husband and wife, they did not need a family counseling agency— there were plenty of aunts or uncles or grandparents who would gladly step in and tell them how to get along with each other. If parents died, a relative took the children into his or her home; an orphanage was not needed.

Too many people are blind to the fact that such conditions no longer exist. They resist expenditures for child welfare services and other social services because they truly believe that families should make do by themselves. The truth is, of course, far different.

The Effects of Urbanization

The United States, like other countries throughout the world, has rapidly become highly urbanized. Few people live on farms. A family is likely to move several times in search of better opportunities while its children are growing up. The extended family of aunts, uncles, cousins and grandparents living close by each other no longer exists. The very demands of industrialization and urbanization to which the family has responded have taken away the family's basic supports, and that is why, in a modern, industrialized, urbanized civilization, social services are not a luxury, but an absolutely essential part of the social fabric. They are as necessary to the community's health as is a clean water system or a good sewage-disposal system—an essential public utility. Unless a people fully recognize this, it is unlikely that they will ever develop a sound national child welfare policy.

Basic to the development of a national policy on child welfare is a country's understanding itself. Only if one knows what is happening, what the impact is on family life and on children of changes within the society, does one learn how to design a child welfare program that meets children's needs.

Lack of Knowledge of Children's Needs

Another reason that the United States has not developed a national child welfare policy is simply lack of knowledge of what children need to grow and develop, lack of knowledge of what poverty of mind and spirit do to the capacity of a child in later life. For example, baby homes or institutions for infants were common in the United States until relatively recently. But as scientific evidence was amassed concerning the needs of the young infant, particularly in regard to stimulation, and as longitudinal research studies established the damage done by poor institutional care, policies changed and infant institutions were either forbidden by law or voluntarily eliminated as their boards recognized that good infant care in institutions was prohibitively expensive.

Recently, the United States developed a large program called Head Start, directed to children of the very poor. It provides for preschool children an enriched educational experience combined with good medical care, nutrition and social services. The program tries to make up for the deprivation that many young children experience when they are reared in homes in which the parents' own background is so deprived or the social pressures are so great that they do not give adequate care, attention and stimulation to the child.

This large program, costing several hundred million dollars a year, came about because child development specialists had gradually amassed research evidence that by age 6—the entrance age to the first grade—many children had fallen so far behind their peers from middle and upper class homes that they never caught up. An important social policy was developed, therefore, out of increased knowledge. This program sometimes comes under attack by those who believe it is too expensive and unjustified.

Regional Disparities

A major factor in the United States that slowed the development of a truly national policy for children was the nature of its political structure. Although the separate states federated rather early in the history of the country—almost 200 years ago—the individual states were nevertheless frequently fiercely independent of each other. Different parts of the country have different traditions, different attitudes. The federal constitution reserved certain responsibilities for people to the federal government, but reserved the bulk of responsibility, particularly for child welfare, to the individual states.

Therefore, as in Australia, there were highly disparate state laws, practices, programs and policies.

In some areas of the country, particularly the Northeast, almost all of the early development of social services was through private agencies, especially those created by churches. In other parts of the country—the Far West and part of the South—governmental agencies came first and relatively few voluntary or private agencies were established.

In some states public agencies subsidize private ones. In others subsidy is unknown and may be expressly forbidden by the constitution of the state. In some states (and again particularly in the eastern part of the country) there was early recognition of the need for social services to protect children, and these states developed such services 100 years before other states. In recent years, great strides have been made toward uniformity of standards throughout the country, primarily as the federal government has assumed a larger and larger share of financial responsibility for social service programs.

The "Invisible Poor"

Another factor that hinders development of a good national policy for children is the very invisibility of the poor child. Michael Harrington, in his book "The Other America," spoke of the "invisible poor." He documented the fact that today in the richer nations most housing, even slum housing, does not look too bad, and slums are usually concentrated in an area of the city or town that one does not have to pass frequently. No one really starves to death—the poor are simply malnourished. No one dies because of lack of medical attention—they just are in poor health because they do not get sufficient or adequate medical attention. The poor multiply and, except to statisticians, the fact that maternal and infant mortality rates may be higher among the poor or that their life expectancy may be much less than that of their more fortunate neighbors, is unknown. Poverty and its effects remain remarkably invisible unless someone makes sure that everyone sees the effects.

Conflicting Attitudes of Professionals

A final obstacle to the development of a national child welfare policy is often, sadly enough, the very people who believe themselves to be doing the most good for children. One of the occupational hazards of working in social welfare is self-righteousness—a belief that, because our motives are unselfish, our opinions and conclusions are above reproach; a belief that, because we are well motivated, we could not possibly possess a vested interest in what we are doing; and finally, a failure to test whether the good things that we are doing are really doing good.

Sometimes public and private agencies subtly war with each other. The private agency thwarts the development of public services because it believes child welfare services to be uniquely the province of the church or a particular private agency. Conversely, a public official may not fully cooperate with private agencies because he envies their ability to choose selectively the families and children they serve, to exclude the very difficult cases, to limit their caseloads, and to enjoy an all-too-pleasant existence, as contrasted with the difficulties of the public official.

Institutional people at times propagandize against the foster home, and those administering foster homes are sometimes not too friendly to the idea of the utility of the institution. Each of us, as research studies have indicated, tends to diagnose the child's needs according to whatever service it is that we have to offer, and are rather blind to the usefulness of other services.

The varying voices of the professionals and their supporting board members often greatly confuse the general public and particularly those, such as legislators, responsible for policy decisions. Good legislation for child welfare is hard enough to get when all of the professionals agree. It is almost impossible to obtain when the professionals are fighting among themselves.

It is also a professional failure, perhaps understandable, to think in too-small terms. When, for example, a person from an agency has been struggling for years to obtain funds to provide day care services for a relative handful of children and out of necessity devises intake policies that exclude all but the most needy children, it is frequently difficult for such a person to think broadly and to advocate day care for all children in need. It is a professional hazard to become inured to scarcity, to be so close to deprivation and so used to it as to accept it. One's sense of anger, of outrage can become dulled.

THE COMPONENTS OF POLICY

What are the components that a child welfare policy must encompass? For an audience as sophisticated as this one, it is a redundancy to enumerate all the various conditions and services that must exist to have strong and healthy families and thus strong and healthy children. In fact, several documents that I have read from the various states, such as a description of child welfare services of the Department of Social Welfare of South Australia, contain the same outline of services that we use at the Child Welfare League or that I have seen used in various European countries. We have come a long way in child welfare internationally to the point of agreement as to what the general scheme of things should look like.

Economic Support

Absolutely basic to the success of any child welfare program is a sound policy of economic support for the family, predicated upon the principle that no child should be allowed to be reared in poverty, with all of the deprivation that that usually entails. First, it should be said that Australia, with its children's allowance system, its widows' pensions and other features, is far more advanced than the United States.

From a child welfare standpoint, economic buttressing of the poor family must be done in such a way that it does not impair the dignity of the family, the self-respect of the child; that it does not single out children as the recipients of the community's charity; and that at a minimum it equalizes educational, health and nutritional standards. Nothing is more foolish than creating expensive palliative child welfare services when it would have been far less costly to support the family financially in the first place. For example, consider the folly of supporting three children from the same family in a children's institution when, had money been given to the mother, she could have supported the children herself in her own home at much less cost and at a greater advantage to the children!

Australia has avoided the absurdities that exist in many other countries, including the United States, by considering separated or divorced women and their children as if the mothers were widowed. Under no circumstances can social services take the place of an adequate family income.

Social Services

The first priority in social services must be those that support or reinforce the ability of parents to meet the children's needs. These services are designed to assist parents with parenting. They include social work services for children in their own homes, including parent-child counseling, marital counseling; protective services for neglected, abused and exploited children; services to unmarried parents; and services designed particularly to assist young mothers in homemaking (including such mundane things as how to budget, how to shop). They also include services designed to assist parents, particularly those from deprived backgrounds, to learn how to help their children develop, how to clothe their children, how to read to them, how to stimulate their interests in the world about them. The harassed urban parent frequently lacks the counsel of his own parents, mature friends and others to assist him.

Services also have to be available to help parents learn how to use community resources. The English call these referral and information services. As life becomes more complex, the community may provide helpful services to parents, but they either do not know about them or do not know how to get them.

Because of the way that various countries develop, it is not uncommon for social services to develop illogically. It seems logical, for example, to provide a homemaker or homehelp aide to go into a home to care for three children when the mother is hospitalized for an extended period or some other family crisis has developed, rather than to place the children in foster care. That seems logical if for no other reason than that the homemaker costs far less than the foster care.

Yet, with the exception of France and one or two other countries, the development has usually been backward. Services to care for children removed from their own homes have been developed long before services to help children in their own homes. Thus, next in the order of priority are services to supplement parental care or compensate for its inadequacies. Among these services are homemaker service for children, various forms of day care, and similar services.

Next, we come to the traditional child care services: foster family care, group home care, institutional care and residential treatment service, and adoption service. These are the services, of course, that have tended to be the first developed in a country, as was the case in Australia. It is not enough simply to list them. A sound policy must be based upon a careful examination of what service is appropriate in what circumstance, and what are the necessary components of each of the services. It is also important to examine which services need to be administered jointly or in the same agency and which can soundly stand alone.

In the United States, we tend to favor the development of multiple-service agencies, that is, agencies that have a wide range of services directed toward the family and children. An agency that has homemakers, children's institutions, foster home care, adoption services and counseling services is far less likely to make an inappropriate choice of service than an agency that has but one form of care. Research studies have clearly indicated that even the well trained professional social worker tends to see the child as needing the service that he or she is administering. There are also important issues to be resolved in relation to the necessary components of any one service.

For example, again in the United States, there are many institutions that do not have proper diagnostic and casework services. They really are not equipped to know what type of child needs their care and they are not equipped to work with the parents of the child to try to restore the child's home or to resolve the difficulties in the situation. There has been a steady move to eliminate this type of child welfare agency and to require by law that all agencies have appropriate casework services, diagnostic services, etc.

Research conducted by the Child Welfare League some years ago clearly indicated that a child's and family's problems must be resolved early during the child's stay in foster care or there will be grave danger that the child will stay indefinitely in foster care. The research finding was that if a child stayed in foster care for 18 months or longer, the odds were he or she would stay there throughout childhood. Intensive help either to assist the family in restoring the child to the family or giving the child up for adoption is needed in a large percentage of foster care cases.

The Agency as Advocate

A necessary part of a child welfare system must also be family and children's agencies' perceptions of themselves as responsible for promoting social action to improve and ensure conditions and services that will promote wholesome child development, strengthen family life, and preserve the child's own home. Agencies must work in the general community to reduce the incidence of circumstances that deprive children of the requirements for their optimal development. Thus, they must serve as spokesmen for children who cannot speak for themselves. They must be "ombudsmen" for children. They must speak out against both private or governmental policies harmful to family life and child life. The reason that this possibility falls upon the social agencies is clear. They are in the best position to see the ill effects of neglect. They have the raw material, the actual cases of children and families, to make real to the public what would otherwise be simply theoretical considerations.

Licensing

Another part of the child welfare system is that of standard setting, licensing, certification, approval of all agencies and facilities providing care and services for children both outside and in their own homes. This is an essential child welfare service that is often neglected.

In some countries, including the United States, there was strong resistance on the part of voluntary agencies to the concept of being licensed by a public agency. As a consequence, in some states there were many exceptions made as to who had to be licensed. Sometimes institutions sponsored by churches or fraternal orders, for example, were exempted. In some states licensing was required only of facilities for children under age 7; in others, only for those over age 7. The principle of licensing should be that all facilities, without exception, must be licensed and must meet standards.

Community Planning

The final component of a good comprehensive system for child welfare is effective community planning for services for children and families. Only through community planning can child welfare services be effectively coordinated with other community resources serving children and families, including income maintenance, family services, health services, mental health services, education, housing, legal and court services, vocational counseling and training, and recreational services.

Child welfare services must mesh with each other. Voluntary and governmental agencies must complement each other. Where there is heavy dependence upon voluntary agencies, planning is necessary to make certain that the agencies together form an effective network of services, instead of an overconcentration in one area and a lack of services in another. The public and private sectors together must see themselves as part of a whole, not as competitors. When there is effective community planning, one can see, for example, voluntary agencies lobbying for and urging sound appropriations for governmental agencies; by the same token, governmental officials may be seen aiding the fund raising of voluntary organizations. Uncoordinated competitive situations can only harm children.

How do we create a national child welfare policy that really protects families and children, that is comprehensive, of high standards, and acceptable to the body politic? Obviously, if I knew the answers I would not be describing the United States in the way that I have been. If you knew the answers, you would not be gathered at this conference. In a sense, there can be no fixed and eternal answers because we are not describing something that is static. A national policy for children must change and evolve as the needs of families change and as our knowledge of what is needed changes. Few things are more dangerous than a rigid blueprint or standards that are not revised periodically.

ACHIEVING A NATIONAL POLICY

Recognizing Deficiencies

The sine qua non for obtaining a national policy for children is, of course, dissatisfaction with the present one or lack of one. Identifying unmet needs; conducting research as to the success and failure of present programs; pinpointing gaps in service; and honestly putting on the table tensions between various sectors of the service network—between public and private, between institutional and noninstitutional service—become important steps to progress. Recognizing deficiencies and being free to talk about them publicly are essential, as is relating cost to the effectiveness of service. All of these are necessary steps along the road.

The general public demands to know whether its money is being spent effectively. There has been too little reporting on the results of family and children's services. Doing so can sometimes lead to dramatic results and meaningful changes in policy.

I can recall debates early in my career in social work about the necessity of having both men and women serve as child care staff in children's institutions. The debate could have gone on forever because the issue was intertwined with vested interests and personal philosophy. A change to a staff of both sexes would have been particularly difficult for institutions run by religious orders of either men or women. A certain institution for delinquent girls commissioned a study to determine the outcome for girls discharged. These girls generally lived in the institution from the time they were committed by the court until age 17, for an average period of 6 years. The institution had a fine educational program, as far as it went. However, the entire program was conducted within the walls of the institution and its staff consisted completely of women. The girls had no contact with men during the period they were in the institution.

The followup study found that a high percentage of the girls were pregnant out of wedlock within 2 years of discharge. The program was changed and men were added to the staff. A subsequent study showed a sharp decline in the number of out-of-wedlock pregnancies. Soon this institution was a leader in obtaining passage of a licensing standard that forbade closed institutions run by adults of one sex.

Developing National Standards

When nations develop as did Australia, and for that matter the United States, over an extremely wide geographic area and under circumstances of great heterogeneity, it is difficult to arrive at a national standard. In the past what happened in one part of the country did not necessarily greatly affect another part because commerce between them was slight. Today, with the tremendous mobility of people, ease of communication and travel, what happens in one town greatly affects another. The care that children receive in Melbourne is of interest to Darwin because some of those children are very likely to live in Darwin as adults. Similarly, Darwin's children may wind up in Melbourne. Thus, it is of concern to an entire nation that services be of high standard throughout the country.

As in the United States, the Australian states are responsible for standards in child welfare, for the administration of licensing laws, and for coordination. In the United States the pressure that led to formation of national standards was the great disparity that existed among the states. The method used by the federal government, which is comparable to your Commonwealth government, to achieve higher child welfare standards in the states was the financial grant with strings attached. Grants were made to the states to improve child welfare services in order to achieve certain standards; unless a state agreed to reach the standards, the grant was not made.

Perhaps the major factor leading to nationally accepted standards was the work of the Child Welfare League of America, created in 1920. It is an association of public and private agencies that banded together to improve the quality of child welfare in the United States. The standards that it developed over the years through committees of experts gradually became the basis for most licensing standards and are often referred to in court decisions affecting foster care, adoption and other children's services. The members of the committees that studied practices and wrote standards represented many disciplines in addition to social work—lawyers, pediatricians, psychiatrists, anthropologists, geneticists, sociologists, and many others. Through national associations, agencies are able to agree upon goals and policies and have a clearer position to enunciate before the public.

Research

Another important factor in arriving at a social welfare policy is the development of research to test the efficacy of children's programs, to identify areas of neglect, to examine public attitudes, etc. For example, in 1950 the Child Welfare League of America commissioned a research study to try to determine why day care was so slow in developing in the United States as compared with other countries. It found a major stumbling block to be public attitudes toward women's employment. People who were opposed to women working were opposed to providing day care for their children and were opposed to good standards. A serious approach had to be made to convince the public of the facts of life concerning working women and children's needs.

Earlier I mentioned another League study that pinpointed needs of children in foster care. That and similar studies provided the basis for a major campaign to obtain massive federal funding for child welfare services. We have found that legislation now in Congress had its origins in such research.

Developing Parent Associations

With some trepidation, child welfare agencies in North America are developing new and powerful allies in attempting to educate the public and develop a saner policy in respect to children. These allies are parents—the parents of children in care, adoptive parents and foster parents. Independent associations of foster parents, guided by and sometimes financed by agencies, have proved a strong force in interpreting foster care and its needs to the general public. Adoptive parent groups, originally critical of agencies and more or less blaming them for lack of children for adoption, have more recently been assisting agencies in getting better legislation, more adequate funding and better understanding of adoption programs on the part of the general public.

Child welfare agencies also find that by bringing representatives of client groups onto their boards, they add a dimension to policy making that never existed before. Clients, frequently from poor and nonwhite groups, often have a perspective markedly different from those of other board members, and at times are more helpful in arriving at a sensible policy in respect to the children under care.

Establishing Legal Rights of Children

Several avenues are being explored to try to create a national child welfare policy. Among them is a new route, establishing the legal rights of children to service. For example, many people believe that if a child needs foster home care, the state does not have a right to limit that care to the amount that it can afford but, under the concept *parens patriae*, must finance the complete cost. Successful legal tests have been made in cases where delinquent children have been sent to so-called training schools. When the schools offered no training, judges have released children, with the logic that the state's right to send a child to a correctional institution is predicated on the state benefiting the child through reeducation, training and therapy. If such services do not exist in the institution, the state has no right to deprive the child of his liberty.

Creating a High Governmental Commission

Another route being pursued today by many organizations, including mental health associations, is that of attempting to obtain the creation of a permanent, high governmental commission on children. Supporters of this proposal believe that because child welfare programs have usually been subordinated to adult programs, a special council or commission on children, based in the President's office, is necessary to serve as a watchdog for children. Its function would be to examine all areas of national life that affect children and to make recommendations to protect them. It would also fight for adequate shares of budgets for family and child welfare.

However, most people believe that the fundamental reason for our not achieving a national policy on children is that the general public does not have a clear understanding of what the components of such a national policy should be. Insufficient effort has been made to gain acceptance of the principles of such a statement as the international "Declaration of the Rights of the Child," adopted by the United Nations, and to translate that statement into terms easily understood by the public.

In spite of modern communication, most people simply do not realize the terrible damage that is done to children by neglect of their maturational needs. To achieve a national policy, we must continue to believe, as I do, that no one deliberately neglects children; no one in his right mind would neglect the future of his country by neglecting its children.

So, the fault must lie with those of us who are charged with responsibility for children. We have somehow not succeeded in our responsibilities to make known their needs; to serve as their spokesmen, their advocates. Most of us have been too complacent in running the programs at hand, in caring for children assigned to us, rather than taking our measure of responsibility for all children. We have not created the sense of urgency that must pervade all of our efforts. Children need what they need when they need it. For them tomorrow is too late.

SAFEGUARDING
THE FAMILY

I have accepted your invitation to come to South Africa and to address this particular subject because I believe we share the common assumption that the key to social stability and national prosperity lies in the stability of the family. Even though my visit has brought me almost to the other side of the world, the many similarities of our two countries bridge the air miles.

The English, with their common-law tradition, and the Dutch, with their Roman system, both shaped the destiny of our respective countries, though at different points in world history. We both subdued the original inhabitants of our countries during periods in our histories, part of which we would prefer to forget.

The original settlers went on to conquer a wilderness, to develop an extremely strong sense of individual worth, of independence, of rugged individualism, and of joining together in a sense of neighborliness and kinship.

For brief periods in the United States we had indentured servitude. For longer and regrettable periods the settlers purchased slaves from the European trading companies whose commerce also set us on the road to industrialization. When slavery was formally abolished, we did not find relief from the problems of a multiracial society based on assumptions of inequality, both real and imagined.

Neither of our countries has devised national policies on racial questions to the satisfaction and well-being of all concerned. We thought we were making positive strides toward racial equality in the United States during the last decade. Indeed, there were many advances toward recognizing the dignity and value of minorities. But, the last few years have not seen a closing of the gap between white and minority incomes.

Presented at the Golden Jubilee Conference, South African National Council for Child Welfare, Pretoria, South Africa, October 1974.

Today we are both strong, highly developed industrialized nations with very high standards of living for part of our populations. We both love sports and the great outdoors of two physically well endowed lands.

There are many other similarities between our two countries because, in part, we share a common heritage. But there are, of course, many, many dissimilarities and I hesitate to draw parallels that will overstate the case. However, as the world has grown smaller, its problems have become more common. The rising expectations of all human beings, the impact of new communication media, such as space-age TV, the mechanization of agriculture, rapidly increasing urbanization, the breakdown of the extended family, and the spector of inflation, affect all of us. It is not mere rhetoric to say that we are all in the same boat, buffeted by the same winds.

The subject, "Safeguarding the Family," can be addressed on many levels. We could, of course, discuss the effects on the family of such factors as human ecology, inflation, expenditures for defense budgets, population growth and stability, and a myriad of other matters that have impact.

My competence, however, lies in other areas. I address you as a social worker whose experience is primarily in the United States, leavened by some years of work with the International Union for Child Welfare in Geneva, of which the South African National Council for Child Welfare is a member.

My knowledge of your country is all too little. Both of our countries have complex problems that are easily misunderstood at a distance. Therefore, I do not want to make assumptions that are incorrect or draw conclusions that are false. For the most part, I will draw upon my experience in the United States; perhaps some of that experience will be germane to South Africa. Some will not, of course.

The Western family has been undergoing major changes in its structure and faces major challenges to its stability. Yet, at least in the United States, recognition of these changes in national social welfare policy is too slow. There is a deeply ingrained reluctance to take steps necessary to safeguard the family. Part of that reluctance is based on a conservative view that the family can and should take care of itself. We tend to preserve a delusion of America as an ever-expanding frontier nation where opportunity is unlimited and where, if a person cannot take advantage of the opportunities, it is because of his innate laziness or incompetence. Somehow, the romantic memories of stalwart men and women traveling by covered wagon to open up the territories of the West exist not only in movies and television, but as a standard when we are writing social welfare legislation.

Many of the economic measures that we have taken to safeguard the family are half-measures, because of a deep fear that if we do too much for the individual and the family, we will promote an unhealthy dependence upon government to solve our problems. The adages of our colonial days, such as "God helps those who help themselves," and "He governs best who governs least," are reflected in our programs.

ESSENTIALITY OF AN ECONOMIC FLOOR

But in spite of such conservative views, the nation has moved to provide the first essential for safeguarding the family, namely, an economic floor. The Great Depression of the 1930s saw the beginning of a national policy of public assistance. First called "Mothers' Aid," then "Aid to Dependent Children," the program significantly was designated later as "Aid to Families With Dependent Children." Eight million children in 3 million families received their basic support through this program in 1973. In most of the families, the father was absent. The average grant to a family was $200 a month; $7.12 billion was spent on this program in 1973.

Yet, in spite of this massive investment and its well intentioned origins, almost all observers believe it to be a failure. The main reason for its failure, in my view, is a defective perception of what is happening to family life in the United States, and an overriding puritanical view that regards the unfortunate as morally defective rather than as victims of the vagaries of our economic system and the development of history.

The program was originally confined to "deserving" families. It was intended for widows with young children whose husbands had died or had become totally disabled. It started, interestingly enough, in the experiment of a children's institution that recognized it might be better for the family, as well as less expensive, to provide an economic subsidy to a home in which the father was dead, rather than bringing the children to live in an institution.

Today few of the children on AFDC are orphans. Like the children we find in our children's institutions and foster homes, they are not orphans of the dead, but orphans of the living. A significant number were born out of wedlock, and a large proportion have fathers who have deserted. Desertion is often referred to as the poor man's divorce, for many men can afford neither legal fees nor child support payments. In over 25% of the families, the fathers simply do not earn as much as the subsistence welfare payments and are eligible, in several states, for supplementation. Almost half of the families receiving public assistance are nonwhite. In other words, AFDC families are no longer the mythological deserving, "ideal" families but, rather, families surrounded by the stigma of illegitimacy, desertion, marital discord, and economic failure—and often of being of the wrong color.

The program is a failure because these millions of families are locked into poverty. Although the grants may seem generous by some standards, in the United States they actually are not because they are below the official governmentally recognized poverty line. This means, of course, that the children in these families live a substandard existence. Their sense of self-worth, of dignity, is vitally damaged by their early perception that the society in which they live views them as less than desirable.

In our case, it is not a question of the U.S. Government's lacking the money to support such families adequately. Rather, we are prisoners of our prejudice and ignorance. In spite of dozens of research studies that have clearly shown that, with very few exceptions, people prefer to work rather than to sit idly on a dole, the public fears that, if grants are adequate, people will not seek employment. In spite of a significant unemployment rate, the general populace still believes that if a man wants a job he can find one. It is the old frontier psychology again. But, of course, there are no more geographic frontiers to conquer in America.

EFFECTS OF MIGRATION AND MOBILITY

It is true that there is still massive migration, however. Several million black citizens have moved from the rural south to the urban north as the mechanization of agriculture has made their labor superfluous. As in Europe, where southern Europeans migrate to northern countries seeking employment, 2 million Puerto Ricans have come to the mainland in search of work, as well as hundreds of thousands of Mexicans. These people have moved not out of laziness, but the opposite. They have uprooted themselves from their homes and friends to seek better economic opportunities elsewhere. The cost to their traditional forms of family life has been tremendous. The resulting cost to the larger society that has to care for the children and mediate the conflicts between generations is beyond measure. Lack of education and salable skills has locked many of these families into urban poverty and consigned them to the slums of our large cities.

In some ways, America as a whole is a migrant society. Fifty years ago a family could expect to stay for a lifetime in the same locality surrounded by relatives. Today a family expects to move several times across state lines or across the country in search of better job opportunities, a better climate or better educational opportunities. And inevitably, the grandparents, aunts, uncles and cousins are left behind or themselves scatter in pursuit of better opportunities.

Almost a quarter of all American families move their households in the course of a year. We must recognize that families who move do so not for selfish reasons but in response to the demands of the economy and the nation. Relocation of industrial plants, planned corporation shifts, military assignment—all demand that the family relocate. In doing so, the family loses many of its own built-in social supports.

The extended family of rural America did not need a community-provided system of social services. Its old-age insurance lay in its many children, who were an economic asset to the farm. It did not need a family counseling agency. The grandmothers and aunts and uncles were all too willing to provide marital counseling to the young in trouble. It had its own day care centers or creches, as the extended family shared in the child-rearing responsibilities. If parents died, other adult members of the family took responsibility for the orphaned children. Divorce, desertion, child neglect were all carefully constrained by the closeness of the family members to each other, by the controls of the churches to which they belonged, by the intimacy and smallness of the communities and neighborhoods in which they lived. Today, most of those influences are seriously weakened or disappearing.

So, when we speak of family supports or of safeguarding the family, we should not be speaking of charitable measures for which a country has an option depending upon the strength of its philan-thropic impulses. Rather, we should be speaking of mandatory supports for the family that are as necessary to the community and nation's health as a clean water supply or an effective transportation system. Instead of "welfare state" being a term of opprobrium, it should be regarded as a description of a sensible society. We cannot leave the safeguarding of the family to the humanitarian impulses of private charity. We have created a society in which the individual family is frequently helpless in the face of the economic and social changes that seem to be never ending.

A fundamental safeguard for the family has to be an assured, decent living standard. If children growing to adulthood are to become useful members of society, they must grow within a family that can surround them with the nurture and protections that every child needs. Attempts to penalize the parents economically for not meeting so-called standards of society will only penalize children and foredoom that society to a dangerous class of misfits—children reared in intolerable circumstances.

It is frequently the economic demands of our society that, perhaps inadvertently, warp family life. It took a long bitter struggle in the United States, as in England, to pass effective laws against child labor. Strong agricultural interests still seek to weaken child labor laws and to permit the employment of very young children in the harvesting of crops. Particularly cruel is the fate of the migrant worker and his family.

Each year, hundreds of thousands of workers, especially on the west and east coasts, follow the harvesting of crops. Since the provision of social and educational services is often geared to local residency, and since the migrant worker is never in one place long enough to obtain residence, the family is often denied even the basic amenities of life. Children go unschooled, have no health facilities, or minimal ones at best, and live in deplorable housing. The workers frequently do not qualify for unemployment insurance. These migrant families do in fact live on the very edge of nonexistence.

Even more destructive of family life in the United States is the situation where male migrants are encouraged to leave their families for months at a time to work in remote areas. Such conditions of employment inevitably destroy family life. They directly promote emotional upheaval for parents and children, contribute to illegitimacy, prostitution, desertion, and child neglect and abuse. Fortunately, we are beginning to pass some laws that forbid this type of exploitation. Corporations requiring such labor are being compelled to build family housing. It is being recognized increasingly that such corporations are profiting from the destruction of family life, and are forcing the general community to assume expenses for family breakdown that are logically a direct charge against the industry that promotes such practices.

We are also gradually overcoming resistance to the setting of standards for social welfare programs by national laws. In the United States, social welfare administration is reserved to the states or local governments. There is growing recognition that what happens to a child in one part of the country can affect the rest of the country, since the child reared in one state is likely to live as an adult in any one of the other 49 states. Thus, there is increasing acceptance of national standards for education, health and social welfare, and national subsidy of local programs to bring them up to such standards.

SUPPORTS TO FAMILIES IN CHILD REARING AND CHILD CARE

Another basic support that a large percentage of families need is assistance in child rearing, particularly when the parents' own background is too limited to permit them to prepare their children effectively for today's educational demands. Recognizing this need, the federal government of the United States established a few years ago a large program called Head Start. It was based on a recognition that by the time a child enters first grade at school it is often too late for him to compete with his peers if his home background has been seriously deprived.

Several million children have benefited from early childhood education. Their parents have been helped to understand the young child's needs by learning to converse with him, to read to him, to observe teachers as they demonstrate ways to stimulate the growth and interest of the young child. The program is, in part, patterned after Israeli experiences, and counterparts may be found in several other countries.

The basic principle to be recognized is that many parents coming from relatively primitive or deprived backgrounds need and want assistance in rearing their young children. In the Head Start program it was found that involvement of the parents was an extremely important measure of the success or failure of the program. It was not a question of someone from the outside doing something to the children but, rather, working with the parents to assist them in their child-rearing responsibilities.

Encouraged by the positive results of Head Start and simultaneously concerned about the lack of education for parenthood, the federal government has taken another positive step. It is funding demonstrations of a systematic, vigorous approach to developing individual and collective competencies to strengthen family life through education and parenthood programs for young people still in secondary school. The appreciation these young students will gain of the needs of children and families in modern society should also create a stronger spirit of child advocacy among them.

A high percentage of Head Start programs have extended their hours so that they also serve as day care centers. Day care has developed rapidly in the United States, but it still a small fraction of what is needed. There are places in day care centers for fewer than one-tenth of the children of working mothers.

Many European countries, particularly the Scandinavian and the eastern European, are far in advance of the United States in their recognition that the stability of the family of the working mother requires adequate day care for her children. Day care centers must not be merely warehouses where children are left during the day; rather, they need to have a stimulating environment conducive to the children's physical, emotional and educational development. For example, the day care center is a logical place to screen young children for health problems and to make early provision for preventive health services. Children's nutrition can be checked and diet supplements provided when necessary. The day care center can also be a place where mothers can be taught good methods of child rearing and education.

Day care, however, should not be seen as simply a service for the children of working mothers. It has many other uses, including daytime care for children of mothers who are ill, or who are heavily burdened emotionally, or whose pressures in their family life are simply so severe that they need respite for part of the day; and even those mothers who recognize that their children need companionship and socialization provided by other children.

Recognizing that the poor family often breaks down under the heavy pressures of modern life, some countries like France have made provisions for low income families to have a free annual vacation at the seaside or another resort area, and do this as a part of their social service system. A few well financed voluntary agencies in the United States are following this lead and are providing summer camp experiences for families.

France is a pioneer in another family support program, namely, homemaker service. Known by various titles, this service provides trained women supervised by social agencies to go into homes to keep them going during periods of unusual stress. A mother may be hospitalized or mentally ill and temporarily out of the home. To strengthen the family and to prevent placement of the children in foster care, a homemaker is provided for the family.

In other countries, including the United States, homemakers assist mothers of deprived backgrounds to learn how to manage a family. They teach budgeting, cooking, child rearing and other essentials.

Increasingly, social agencies are trying to find ways to help families overcome the isolation in which a typical family of husband and wife and two children find themselves when they are hundreds of miles away from any relatives. Traditional programs, such as family counseling and marital counseling, are being supplemented by workers called family advocates, who help families with their difficulties with the governmental and corporate bureaucracies. They help families with their housing problems or guide them to work-training programs. They assist families to combat gouging landlords and help them to build strengths against impersonal school boards that may be providing deficient education.

ROLE OF BUSINESS AND INDUSTRY

Many business corporations are helping to safeguard family life by, for example, offering female employees the option of working shifts that coincide with the school hours of their children. During the summer they permit these women to take their vacations at the same time as their husbands do, or permit summer leaves of absence so that the mothers can be home with their children during the school vacation. The corporations employ students to take the place of these women during their leaves of absence. This is one small example of an approach to alleviate the burden of working mothers.

Paid maternity leave, common in some European countries, is just beginning to be recognized in the United States. Happily, three or four big companies are extending maternity leave to adoptive parents so that these mothers, too, may be at home with their new children.

In other words, business corporations are recognizing the fact that they cannot ignore the parental responsibilities of working parents. They are beginning to see that enabling a working mother to take time off to be with her sick child is essential to the health of the family and the health of the community. Instead of threatening such a mother with dismissal, they set up personnel policies that not only permit such an absence but encourage it.

Another encouraging new move on industry's part is provision of family counseling services as a fringe benefit. Companies achieve this by contracting with a local family service agency. The contracting social agency sends experienced counselors to the plant on specified days and the company takes the responsibilty of lining up appointments on request from employees. An employee need only ask for an appointment, and he is given the necessary time off. The employees and the companies are finding this new move to be mutually satisfactory.

Very slowly nations are coming to the realization that social practices that weaken the family inevitably cost many times more for later remedial work on damaged children and rebellious adults than the cost of measures that support the family. Fortunately, too, the workers themselves are seeing the ill effects of pursuing economic advancement at the expense of their families. For example, several large corporations in the United States have recently reported that many young executives are refusing to accept frequent transfers to other communities in order to obtain advancement. Their blunt answer is that they cannot move every 2 years without hurting their family life, their children's education, etc. The corporations themselves are gradually seeing the same thing. Family breakdown and marital discord that frequently accompany such mobility in the end cost far more than any temporary gains for the corporation.

SERVICES FOR VULNERABLE FAMILIES

In many countries services are rapidly developing to protect the family that is particularly vulnerable. For example, throughout the western world unwed mothers are increasingly keeping their children instead of placing them for adoption. In some northern European countries as many as 95% of all unwed mothers retain their children. In the United States there has been a drop of two-thirds in children released for adoption in a 4-year period.

These mothers without husbands need special protection if the families they are creating are to be viable. In some of the Scandinavian countries special housing programs, free medical programs and special training programs are provided for them.

An unfortunate trend is the increasing percentage of mothers who bear children during adolescence. Such young women are often ill equipped to rear children. There is a high percentage of divorce, child abuse and other negative social indicators among such families. Although there is resistance to programs to aid unwed mothers because of puritanical fears, there is a marked growth of courses in public secondary schools to educate young people in marriage, sex and child rearing.

Family breakdown frequently occurs when the strains of rearing a severely retarded or otherwise handicapped child become too great for the family. Instead of simply providing special programs for such handicapped children, some countries are seeing the wisdom of attempting to prevent mental retardation.

In Sweden not only is the medical care free, but all mothers are paid a fee for attending prenatal clinics. The motivation behind such programs is not philanthropic. It is clearly evident that it is cost-effective to provide free prenatal care to assure adequate nutrition of the mother as a means of preventing the birth of children who are mentally retarded.

I would like to end my remarks with an observation on a change that I think lends the greatest hope for safeguarding the family. That change is a slowly developing recognition that it is not possible for any country to try to safeguard part of its families. It is all or nothing. *No family is safe, no child is safe, while another family, another child remains unguarded.* There is no real security for any family if it must live in fear—for fear takes a terrible toll in human spirit. We are learning this in the United States as we have experienced the impact on our society of decades of neglect of millions of poor families. Rising crime rates, social unrest, deterioration of our cities and social life are the direct result of our neglect, and we are paying for that neglect in greatly increased taxes and other necessary expenditures.

It cannot be stressed forcefully enough that safeguarding *all* families is a responsibility for society as a whole. We have seen in our country the results of ignoring a problem because it was thought to be peculiar to a minority racial group and, therefore, not of great concern.

Heroin use was a common element among a subculture of black ghetto youths and jazz musicians. The larger society ignored it and it spread until one day the sons and daughters of white middle class families, who did not come from an economically deprived background, were junkies hooked on heroin. The crime rate associated with hard drug usage and the loss in productivity to society are now astronomical.

It is not charity or philanthropy that should motivate us in providing the economic support and the social services required to strengthen today's families; rather, the motivation should be that we cannot afford to do anything else. For in this deeply troubled world with its competing political and economic ideologies, its nuclear power races, and its myriad bitter struggles, the nations that will probably survive in the end will be those that have made sure that all of their children will be nurtured to strength within secure and dignified families.

This Golden Jubilee Conference is a search to better protect the citizens of tomorrow. Unfortunately, I come from a country that is well down the list of countries when they are measured against their efforts to safeguard family life. We must not be afraid to look everywhere for better methods of helping the family. We share a fear of communism, but I want to point out that some of the socialist countries of Eastern Europe have developed far superior programs for safeguarding the family than we have in the United States. Emphasis upon high quality and universally available day care is one example.

The Scandinavian countries have produced excellent programs of health protection for the family and have gone far in ridding themselves of nonfunctional concepts, such as illegitimacy. England's referral and information bureaus and multiservice agencies are valuable in protecting family life. Israel's experiments in helping its Oriental families, who come from a 14th century environment of northern Africa, adjust to 20th century life, are worthy of study. France's extended insurance program against unemployment will do much to strengthen family life. China's rural cooperatives, Canada's children's allowance system—all provide important examples for our countries.

It has been said that the root of civilization can be traced to the smallest cooperative human efforts. No man can live alone, isolated from his neighbor. Throughout history we have seen civilizations that were once strong fall because they forgot that basic rule and chose instead paths of divisiveness and greed. The "haves" can withhold from the "have nots" only at their own peril. We need to put our efforts into reaching out to support the vulnerable members of our society if we wish to be able to discuss the family in any meaningful terms in years to come.

II.

INTERDEPENDENCE OF PUBLIC AND VOLUNTARY AGENCIES

THE ROLES OF PUBLIC AND PRIVATE AGENCIES IN PROVIDING SERVICES TO CHILDREN

When there has been so much written about this subject in the past, why is it that, at the first Arden House Conference on child welfare, the subject of private and public agency relationships should be addressed again? I believe the reason is that, in the last few years, there have been several major changes in attitudes of such magnitude that we need to look afresh at public and private relationships. These changes include:

1) the growing acceptance of a welfare state philosophy in the United States;

2) the growing security of minority religious groups;

3) a realistic acceptance of the fact that private philanthropy is unable to provide coverage services in child welfare; and

4) progress in racial equality.

ACCEPTANCE OF A WELFARE STATE PHILOSOPHY

Our last national election and recent acts of Congress have seemed to settle once and for all the issue of whether the American people wish government to be used as the basic method of assuring security to the individual, or as the last-resort instrumentality to be used only when everything else has failed. In short, the American people have accepted the desirability of the welfare state. This, of course, does not mean an end to the great debate over local versus state versus federal responsibility, or rugged individualism versus a

Presented at the Arden House Conference on Child Welfare Services, Harriman, New York, November 3, 1965.

planned economy. Nor does it mean that we will immediately use the full potential of the federal government to eradicate human want. But, in my opinion, it does mean that there will be a steady and inexorable increase in the assumption of public responsibility for services designed to protect the individual and the family.

The 1962 Social Security Amendments, for example, settled in principle that public child welfare services should be available in all counties to all children in need of them. The Medicare bill, the Economic Opportuntiy Act, the various education bills—all are of fundamental significance.

Not only has there been a change in attitude in respect to the use of federal taxing power for the public welfare, but particularly within the Economic Opportunity Act there has been a change in the historic relationship of the federal government to state and local communities. For the first time, at least in the welfare field, the federal government is dealing directly with local communities as distinguished from working solely with government at the state level. This factor alone is already creating sweeping changes in the programs of hundreds of voluntary agencies.

GROWING SECURITY OF RELIGIOUS MINORITIES

The second major change that has characterized the last few years is the growing security of minority religious groups, which is reflected in a changing attitude of sectarian agencies toward public child welfare. A large proportion of child welfare services had their origin in the concern of religious groups for the welfare of children. There are hundreds of sectarian organizations in the child welfare field today. Catholics and Jews and, to a lesser extent, Protestants, have long believed that the protection of the child's religious heritage and culture can best be provided by sectarian agencies. Jews and Catholics tended to develop total coverage programs designed to provide care for every child of their faith. Elements of all religious groups feared expansion of direct public services.

Catholic leadership, which was both better organized and more articulate than that of other groups, presents the best illustration of this viewpoint and its transition. Its philosophy was well stated by Father (now Bishop) Thomas Gill in the Social Work Yearbook of 1961 (pages 83-84):

Of late years a consensus has been forming among the leadership in Catholic child care that considerations of substantial importance to the survival of high standards of child welfare urge continuation of responsibility by religious bodies, not only for specialized, experimental services, but for the broad program of foster care. That conviction stems primarily from the frank recognition that some interests of children have not been adequately served by agencies either not situated or not equipped to give such interests due emphasis.

Since private sources could not finance a coverage service of foster care, religious groups had a keen interest in preserving and expanding governmental support of private child welfare agencies. When, in 1950, the Child Welfare League of America issued a statement on principles and policies of voluntary child welfare agencies that 1) contained a stricture against lump-sum subsidy to private agencies; 2) advocated purchase of care on a case-by-case basis; and 3) called for an expansion of public services, Monsignor Thomas O'Grady, Secretary, National Conference of Catholic Charities, stated the following in a letter sent to all governors and public welfare directors in the United States:

Not only will the Statement issued by the Child Welfare League affect the traditional relationships between voluntary agencies and the local government in the care of children for whom government has been making payments; it will affect the care of all children. Public services are to be made available to all children for whom their families are unable to provide proper care or services. Governmental agencies will thus be in the entire field of child welfare. They will secure federal funds to help them, not only in taking care of needy children, but in providing services for all children, independent of need. This is the new Utopia to which the Child Welfare League of America is pointing. It means fairly complete control by the national government over all individual and family life.

In the experience of the years that followed, fears of control by government were somewhat allayed. Purchase of care on a case-by-case basis was not found to disadvantage the private agency, and the disparity between need and the ability of either public or private agencies to meet that need became more apparent.

In 1959 Secretary Arthur S. Fleming, Secretary of Health, Education, and Welfare, appointed an Advisory Council on Child

Welfare Services to examine Part 3 of Title V of the Social Security Act. The major recommendation of the Council was that the federal government pay part of the total cost of public child welfare services, through federal grants-in-aid on a variable matching basis with an open-end appropriation. In supporting this recommendation, Monsignor Raymond Gallagher (now Bishop Gallagher), who represented the National Conference of Catholic Charities, stated:

> A primary means of extending public welfare services to children in urban areas (should be) the purchasing of service from voluntary agencies and institutions on a case-by-case, cost-of-care basis.[1]

The fact that the representatives of the three major religious groups who served on the Advisory Council supported the recommendation for federal sharing of direct cost of child welfare services marks a major evolution in the philosophy of religious groups toward public child welfare.

Testimony confirming this change came during the Congressional hearings on the Social Security Amendments of 1962. The Administration bill had proposed that purchase of service be used widely as a means of carrying out provision of services to public assistance clients. Jewish, Protestant and Catholic spokesmen all testified to the effect that private funds should constitute the major part of a private agency's income. Speaking to that section of the bill that would have permitted the purchase of service from private agencies, Monsignor Gallagher stated:

> We further recommend that wherever it is prudent to do so, public welfare administrators should purchase service from private agencies and institutions where this service can be effectively rendered by this means. We believe that purchase-of-service agreements should be on a per diem, per capita, item-by-item basis. We further believe that purchase of service should not constitute the greater part of the income of an agency. Voluntary private welfare service should continue to bear the responsibility for raising more than half of its income by voluntary giving, so that the precise mission of voluntary groups might be continuously preserved: namely, the active participation of the individual citizens in helping to meet the needs of their fellow citizens by reasons of their personal efforts and contributions.[2,3]

In principle, the testimony of the National Council of Churches and other groups was in concurrence on the point that the major source of funding of private agencies should be through voluntary contributions.

In my view, it is difficult to overestimate the significance of the testimony of the religious groups in regard to purchase of service. In essence, it marked the giving up of the concept that child welfare services under religious auspices must be total coverage services, and implied an acceptance of direct public services.

There is other evidence to support this point. In many large cities and states, sectarian agencies—Protestant, Catholic and Jewish—have been and are actively supporting the development of direct public services. Jewish agencies in several cities have transferred their foster family care load to public agencies. Directors of Catholic charities in many cities have made it clear that they no longer can provide care for all Catholic children. In fact, one has to go back several years for examples of sectarian groups openly attempting to block the expansion of public child welfare services.

What accounts for this change? There are, of course, many reasons. But is seems to me that the major factor has been the lessening of religious prejudice in the United States, the growing political equality of minority religious groups, the rapid elimination of nationality and religious ghettos.

Another element in this change of attitude by religious groups was a reciprocal change in the attitude of public welfare administrators toward private agencies.[4] I comment later on this point.

LIMITATIONS OF PRIVATE PHILANTHROPY

The third factor that makes for a fruitful reexamination of relationships between public and private agencies is a frank recognition that private philanthropy cannot do the job. Just a few years ago, one of the most common unofficial campaign slogans of community chests and United Funds was "Give—in order to prevent government from developing social welfare programs." This appeal is heard far less frequently today. Again, this is probably a reflection of the changing attitude in the United States toward the welfare state. In part, however, it is also a recognition of the magnitude of need and of the failure of community chest funding for child welfare agencies, at least, to keep pace with the growing population and the increased costs of providing services. In spite of the fact that each year the total number of dollars raised in the United States increases, there has been little increase in the amount of child welfare services provided through private agencies. Almost all increase of service has taken place in the public sector. Persons of good will, no matter how committed to the concept of private philanthropy, cannot overlook the apparent impossibility of private funds' financing total-coverage services.

Therefore, in community planning associated with United Funds and community chests, there is a far more active search for a definition of the unique role of voluntarism.[5]

PROGRESS IN RACIAL EQUALITY

The final major factor that makes it fruitful to reexamine public-private relationships is the racial revolution. The child welfare field has not escaped the disease of the rest of our culture—racial prejudice. Although the field deplored the fact that services were so often unavailable to nonwhite groups, nevertheless it failed to provide sufficient services. It was "explained," for example, that the black unmarried mother could not obtain services because there were no foster homes or adoptive homes available for her child. Agencies might say they wished they could accept blacks into their institutions, but then added that the community would not permit it. Today there is not the least shadow of doubt that services must be provided for nonwhite groups on the same basis as for white groups. To accomplish this end may necessitate at least a 50% increase in available child welfare services. Inevitably, this means a reexamination of public-private roles. Both sectors of the child welfare system must move to meet the need.

In summary, it is not mere rhetoric to say that this is the time for a basic reexamination of public-private agency roles. That examination can be meaningful because we are close to reaching a consensus. We can examine the blocks to better public-private relationships because it is obvious that they have to be improved. We can examine respective roles because it is obvious that the public and private sectors cannot play the same roles. The Board of Directors and the Advisory Council of Executives of the Child Welfare League of America have voted to undertake a restudy of principles and policies in administration of voluntary and public child welfare agencies because they are convinced, in light of these historic changes, that the statement of the League in 1958 is now outmoded.

Certain factors must be taken into account as we move to reexamine the roles of public and voluntary agencies.

DIVERSE PATTERNS OF PUBLIC-PRIVATE RELATIONSHIPS

First, it is obvious that there are such diversities in the present roles of public and private agencies in the United States that it is difficult to generalize as to the present, let alone to prescribe a future. Expenditures of state and local public funds per capita for child welfare are 50 times as high in New York ($10.82 per child) as in Texas (24 cents per child). If children in their own homes are excluded, approximately 55% of all children served are served by public agencies and 45% by private, but in some states almost all services are given by private agencies, and in others, most are given by public.

If we look at specific functions, the diversity is even greater. In the nation as a whole, 86% of all institutional care is provided by private agencies. Twenty states have no public institutional care at all. In Ohio, however, more than 60% of all institutional care is provided by public agencies. Other statistics clearly indicate that factors other than professional standards and convictions have influenced the development of child welfare services.

Of all dependent and neglected children outside their own homes, 70% are cared for in foster family care and 30% in institutions. In Texas 80% are in institutions, while in Maryland 88% are in foster homes, and Utah reports all children in foster homes. If diversity within a plural structure is considered a virtue, then child welfare is very virtuous indeed.

National averages are also deceptive when it comes to analyzing purchase-of-care arrangements. Nationally, 42% of all governmental funds spent on foster care are devoted to purchase of care from private agencies. However, Mississippi spends nothing for purchase of care, while New York devotes 76% of its expenditures to purchase of care. If you come from Arkansas, you are likely to think of adoption as wholly a public service, since almost 100% of adoptive placements are made by public agencies, while in North Dakota 99% are made by voluntary agencies.

The only neat statistic I can find is in the area of maternity home care. Nationally, 100% of all maternity home care is given by private agencies.[6]

Such diversity requires us to be careful in attempting to apply a general principle across the field. For example, the concept that no more than 50% of a private agency's funds should come from public sources, if immediately put into effect, would produce chaos. A high percentage of private institutions are dependent upon public funds for their continuance, and in many cases, public funds amount to far more than 50% of the private institution's budget. We do need, however, to examine carefully whether providing institutional care almost wholly through private agencies is sound or unsound. On one hand, there is evidence that children are more likely to get the service they need when an agency has multiple services. If public agencies lack institutional services, are they making sound use of them? If private agencies have institutional services, it may well be that children are being placed in institutions who do not benefit from that type of care.[7] On the other hand, there is evidence that institutional care can be less expensively provided by private agencies than public.[8] Furthermore, the 24-hour care of children in institutions, of necessity, involves the religious upbringing of children. It may not be possible for public agencies to provide such service adequately.

Another example is seen in protective services. Until recently, most protective services were provided by private agencies in the few cities where they existed at all. Yet it has long been obvious that it is not possible for private agencies to finance communitywide protective services. They *must* be developed under public auspices. In my view, any existing programs or demonstrations of protective services under private auspices must have as their primary goal the establishment of the function within public agencies.

ESSENTIALITY OF PRIVATE SERVICES

Before proceeding further, I must make clear my conviction that a strong sector of private services in the child welfare system is absolutely essential to the proper development and growth of child welfare services and the protection of children. Public and private agencies *do* have different characteristics, different advantages and disadvantages. In general, the private agency, potentially at least, can move its feet faster, be more selective, go farther out on the limb, and is essentially a more flexible instrument. Furthermore, the vital function of a "yardstick" should not be overlooked. Monopoly in any field is dangerous. It is doubly so in child welfare, where we are really only at the beginning of knowledge. Parallel services, therefore, are not necessarily duplication. They are frequently essential to the health of both public and private agencies.

It follows that I believe it to be in the vital interest of both public and private agencies that public and private services in such areas as adoption, foster family home care, treatment of disturbed children, day care and institutional care be maintained. In addition to the many other reasons, maintaining private services is a valid objective of purchase of service.

DISTRUST BETWEEN PUBLIC AND PRIVATE AGENCIES

As we seek to make more rational the roles of public and private agencies, we must face frankly the mutual fear, suspicion and hostility that still exist in some measure between public and private agencies. It is pleasanter to talk about the cooperativeness and mutual respect between public and private agencies, and, of course, one can find many examples of cooperation. However, it is more important, I believe, to accept the fact that hostility does exist, identify the factors that have created it, and seek to eliminate them. Among these factors are the following:

1) The superior attitude that private agency personnel evidence toward public agency personnel. Private agencies do have a larger percentage of trained personnel. Because they can close or limit intake, they tend to have lower caseloads, and in other areas they can point to certain criteria of alleged quality of service. Too often, however, instead of identifying their advantages, they have simply "crowed" about their superiority. Necessarily, this has not endeared them to public agency personnel.

2) Public and private agencies seldom come to each other's support. How often has a public agency appeared before a budget committee of community chest to testify for a more adequate budget for a private child welfare agency? How often do private agency executives testify before public budget hearings for more adequate funds for public child welfare, except to ask for higher payments for purchase of care? How many private agency executives really involve their boards in a concern for all child welfare services, instead of concentrating only on the interests of their own agency? In how many states does the state welfare department involve private agencies in devising its annual child welfare plan? How many times has a public agency announced without prior consultation with private agencies that it was going to provide a service—to the damage of private

agency fund raising and planning? In how many communities has a private agency closed intake without prior consultation with the public agency, which must inevitably take on the children the private agency has closed out? How many private agency executives have subtly or not so subtly lobbied against public services by saying that services can be provided on a quality basis only by private agencies? Lobbying for a law such as the one in Chicago that required the public agency to certify that no private agency would accept the child before it could provide care was not exactly conducive to building sound private-public relationships.

At this time of rapid governmental expansion, the public agencies' attitude toward private agencies is crucial. Many public welfare administrators are basically contemptuous of the role and importance of the private agency. If public agencies truly believe that the voluntary agency is essential in our pluralistic society, they must be imaginative in seeking ways to strengthen and further develop the voluntary agency. If, however, they pay only lip service to the ideal, they can aid in its destruction.

Many of the conditions that led to mutual distrust are disappearing, and others can be overcome. For example, there is a serious imbalance in the distribution of scarce professional personnel. We have long concentrated on standards that identify the minimum of professional personel necessary to provide a sound service. Little has been done, however, to identify maximum ratios of professional personnel. I think it is vital that agencies such as the Child Welfare League, in carrying out their accrediting function, not accredit an agency that has more professional personnel than the volume of its services requires or justifies. Instead of a private agency's being proud that *all* of its personnel are trained, its boast should be that it uses professionals only on tasks requiring them and thus does not monopolize professional workers unnecessarily.

THREATS TO VOLUNTARISM

It is essential that we maintain not merely nongovernmental agencies but *truly voluntary* agencies. Samuel Mencher has cogently analyzed factors in the development of private social work that have tended to eliminate opportunities for true voluntarism.[9] Among them are the professionalization and bureaucratization of voluntary social agencies, and the resultant declining role of meaningful activity for the volunteer.

Although many child welfare agencies make good use of volunteers, most agencies do not. It is true that almost all voluntary social agencies have boards of directors, but a common complaint of such boards is that they no longer have the direct "feel" of the service, and that they are too often "rubber stamps" for the paid staff. Fortunately, there has been a recent renewal of interest in making more effective use of volunteers. But rarely is the need for volunteer activity seen as basic to the survival of the private agency.

In trying to draw a line between policy making and administration in the provision of professional services, too many social work administrators have, sometimes inadvertently, excluded the volunteer from a real sense of identification and participation in the agency's services. As a consequence, the volunteer frequently loses his enthusiasm for the private agency as a volunteer service, and is perfectly willing to permit "government to take over."

The United Fund and Federation movement has perhaps unwittingly aided and abetted the removal of the volunteer from a meaningful relationship with agencies. Mencher has pointed out that, generally speaking, the more complex and the larger an organization, the more difficult it is to provide a meaningful and effective experience for the volunteer. Yet organized community planning in most communities, perhaps frustrated by attempts to meet needs, frequently concentrates on problems of organization, with pressure for mergers and for the creation of ever-larger private welfare units the usual result.

Many United Funds have also shown a deplorable tendency to take away from individual agency boards even their policy-making functions and to consolidate these functions in the United Fund hierarchy. Perhaps the ultimate of such attempts was reached in one major western city where the United Fund required that it review every individual employee's increment in salary proposed by any agency in the United Fund.

Voluntary agencies should reflect the differences within our society. As meaningful policy making is removed from the individual agency board, the agency becomes less and less a viable expression of voluntarism.

Fortunately, within the United Fund and community chest movement there are leaders who clearly see that the health of voluntary agencies depends upon freedom and independence within reason, and who strive to maintain maximum autonomy for each private agency. There is also, within the United Funds, leadership that is fighting against the tendency of United Funds to become simply givers' protective leagues. Coercive compulsion on the individual to contribute to a monolithic United Fund, or coercive restrictions on agencies that prevent them from expanding their services through supplemental fund raising, are inimical to the welfare of voluntarism. It can well be argued that the future health of voluntary child welfare agencies, as well as other private agencies, depends not upon a more and more efficient United Fund but upon the loosening of the United Fund structure. We need more, not less, diversity in fund raising—more, not fewer, appeals to the public conscience. More competition, if you will.

IMPORTANCE OF CITIZEN INVOLVEMENT

It must be stated that it is the voluntary agency that has provided citizen involvement in child welfare. Public agencies by and large have failed to use volunteers or even to permit citizen involvement. There is resistance in public welfare, for example, to citizen advisory boards. The higher the level of government, the more fear there seems to be of citizen participation.

The future development of good child welfare services in part depends upon the professional's ability to enable volunteers to develop firsthand knowledge of the problems that face the country. There is no substitute for direct experience. There are ways in which child welfare agencies, public and private, could increase the opportunities of volunteers for such experience today. For example, some years ago a proposal was made that guardianship of dependent children not be placed solely in the hands of the agencies caring for them. In addition to the agency, it was proposed that an individual be designated as the child's guardian. I believe this idea has great merit. I suggest that every child who requires a guardian should have dual guardians, an agency and an individual volunteer who has no official or formal connection with the agency. The volunteer should be drawn from a pool of concerned volunteers who would agree to serve as coguardians of the child. The agreement should be so drafted that the individual guardian does not have financial responsibility for the child. His duties would consist of being aware of the child's circumstances and intervening on his behalf, where appropriate. He would be concerned, for example, if his child were re-placed many times while in foster care or if he stayed on in foster care when he should be placed for adoption. The guardian would inform himself on the quality of care, including educational opportunities, medical care, etc.

To the agencies, such a system might constitute an overwhelming nuisance. It would introduce a fourth dimension to the already complicated triangle of child welfare agency, foster parent and natural parent. However, I think the advantages of such a system would outweigh the disadvantages. What might be the result of having a cadre of volunteer guardians who are well informed about the conditions of foster care today, who are aware of the high caseloads, of foster home turnover, of inadequate payments to foster parents, of poor institutional programs?

Such a group would present a powerful volunteer force to improve child welfare generally. One of the weaknesses of any bureaucracy or of any profession is that it becomes too accustomed or perhaps too resigned to its own limitations. What we may regard as the inevitable weakness of our programs, a volunteer citizen responsible as a child's guardian might not take for granted.

The United States is often thought of as the country that has developed the widest variety of agencies. It is interesting to note that, in many countries where services have been primarily provided by government, private services are now developing at the instigation of government. Japan is one such country. And even in the Communist countries, there is a recognition of the value of voluntary citizen effort. Mencher has pointed out that in Great Britain the strongest support for private agencies comes from public welfare officials. The same observation can be made about Denmark and other European countries.

In summary, I believe we have reached the time at which there can be a most fruitful examination and determination of the respective roles of public and private agencies.

Overcoming old attitudes and prejudices inappropriate to a new reality will be the prerequisite to maintaining a strong system of child welfare provided by public, sectarian and voluntary nonsectarian services. If private agencies are freed of their fear that they will be put out of business by the growth of public agencies, freed of their compulsion to hold on to a service, and committed to the ideal of promoting voluntarism, perhaps they can become the experimental, demonstrating, flexible organizations that they should be. Perhaps then they can serve to pioneer in the development of services that ultimately will be recognized by the public and assumed as a public function. And then we can get on with the job spelled out in the 1962 Amendments to the Social Security Act of making child welfare services available to every child in need.

REFERENCES

1. Report of the Advisory Council on Child Welfare Services, U.S. Department of Health, Education, and Welfare, U.S. Government Printing Office, Washington, D.C., 1960.
2. Hearings before the Committee on Ways and Means, House of Representatives, 87th Congress, Second Session, on H.R. 10032, February 7, 9 and 13, 1962, U.S. Government Printing Office.
3. Although Monsignor Gallagher was the spokesman for the National Conference of Catholic Charities, it should be pointed out that a spokesman for the New York State Catholic Welfare Conference in essence did not support this aspect of Monsignor Gallagher's testimony.
4. Ellen Winston. "A New Era of Partnership in Services for Children," *Child Welfare*, XLIII, 5 (May 1964), 221.
5. See the United Community Funds and Councils' 1965 study on voluntarism.
6. Caution must be used in analyzing statistics in the child welfare field. The most comprehensive data available come from the U.S. Children's Bureau, but many of its statistics are imperfect, since many states do not collect statistics. Furthermore, the Children's Bureau uses a definition that excludes child welfare services rendered by any public agency other than the public welfare department, and in some states a large percentage of child welfare services are provided by juvenile courts and other governmental agencies.
7. Scott Briar. "Clinical Judgment in Foster Care Placement," *Child Welfare*, XLII, 4 (April 1963), 161.
8. Lydia Hylton. *The Residential Treatment Center: Children, Program and Costs*, New York: Child Welfare League of America, 1964.
9. Samuel Mencher. "The Future for Voluntarism in American Social Welfare, in *Issues in American Social Work*, Alfred J. Kahn, editor. New York: Columbia University Press, 1959, 219–241.

SOME OBSERVATIONS ON PRIVATE CASEWORK AGENCIES AND SOCIAL POLICY

The premise of this conference is that currently social work is not making as great a contribution to the development of social policy as it could and, further, that is has lost some of its early impetus toward social action. It is also assumed that schools of social work are not preparing students to function effectively in this area.

The writer concurs with this premise. However, I do not agree with those who believe that social workers have almost wholly abdicated their responsibility for development of a progressively enlightened social policy and for taking part in effective social action to translate policy into program. One need only compare the quality of social service programs in the private field today with the quality of those of 30, 20 or even 10 years ago to realize that consistent progress has been made. For example, the child welfare field, the area with which I am most familiar and will use for reference, has shown remarkable change as viewed in historical perspective.

Child care has changed from an essentially custodial, institutional focus to a multiservice "treatment" orientation. A new social policy is reflected in increasing awareness in the community of the needs of the emotionally disturbed child; recognition of adoption as a solution for the unattached child; perception of short-term foster home care as the basic service for children cared for outside their own homes; and, finally a sharp reorientation toward the place of the family in the child's life.

Presented at the Arden House Conference on Social Policy and Social Work Education, Harriman, New York, April 22–25, 1957.

However, it must be admitted that this achievement can be attributed less to a conscious assumption by most social workers of professional responsibility for development of improved social policy, than to accidents of personality, namely, having in the right job at the right time a person with a flair for effecting change. Perhaps of greater concern than what has or has not been achieved is the fact that the average caseworker does not view as one of his skills, duties and responsibilities the continuing development of progressive social policy. Fortunately, it is precisely this lack that can be corrected by adequate education.

PRIVATE AGENCIES' NEED FOR HELP

Perhaps the most clear-cut evidence of the need of private agencies for help in this area is the tremendous disparity between what has long been known and recognized *within the profession* as basic minimum standards for the healthy development of families and children, and the extent to which these have been achieved. As testimony, we offer the following simple but frequently quoted statistics: only 5% of American cities have minimally adequate services for the unmarried mother; thousands of children spend time in common jails each year in our country; more than 40% of America's 1400 private children's institutions still give 24-hour care to preschool children, despite clear scientific evidence of the damaging effect of such care; more than three-quarters of the child welfare agencies in the United States have no casework services; in most communities there is a paucity of services for the child with personality problems, a lack of child guidance clinics, treatment centers and school guidance facilities.

Although it is uncommon to find a private casework agency that is unconcerned with basic social conditions as they exist within the community, the general inadequacy of public social welfare services and the limitations of their own intake policies, it is extremely common to find private agency staff who have only a hazy idea of such vital facts as who their Congressman is, what the level of ADC grants is in their community, the legal base of public assistance, and similar data. Moreover, only a small percentage of private agencies have a board committee on legislation. Still fewer invest any considerable time in educating their board members, let alone the general community, about anything beyond the narrow function of their agency.

This situation exists even though social work, more than any other profession, is almost wholly dependent upon public understanding if it is to be effective. It exists despite the fact that the laymen who serve on boards of private agencies, and whose number is estimated to be between 80,000 and 100,000 in casework agencies alone, should be the most effective nucleus for the development of good social policy in the United States. To many boards it comes as a surprise that one of their primary responsibilities, in serving as stewards of the community, is developing and gaining acceptance of good social policy.

Why do these conditions exist? The "whys" have been frequently analyzed over many years. Little can be said on the subject that has not already been said in professional papers at national conferences on social work. Recent developments, however, have made some of these "whys" more obvious.

CHANGING FOCUS OF PRIVATE AGENCY PROGRAMS

The evolution of private agencies has been a major cause. Private agencies are, by their own definition, specialized, experimental, limited in scope—the product of the right of choice of a few individuals to serve a certain segment of human need. This is not in itself bad. Overwhelmed by the mass problems of the depression of the 1930s, the private family agencies had to leave the field of financial assistance. Because of rapidly growing population and the tremendous increase in costs forced by intensification of program, the private child welfare agencies have yearly dealt with fewer and fewer children on a more intensive basis.

Many ills of the human personality can by no means be solved solely by better housing, better economic conditions, good food or better clothing. It is good, therefore, that private agencies have responded so notably to modern scientific knowledge emanating from the fields of psychiatry and psychology. However, as they have recognized the seriousness of emotional malnutrition, they have also come to believe that it is more intellectually stimulating to attempt to overcome than is physical malnutrition. Increased knowledge concerning the prevention and treatment of emotional disturbances has necessitated intensifying the skills of social workers who would deal with them. In concentrating on the development of these skills, a large proportion of caseworkers have turned exclusively to the inward facets of human problems, rather than the broader aspects that concerned their forebears in social work. Since most administrators are recruited from casework ranks, this emphasis in training has conditioned their functioning and interest.

Many private casework agencies have, on their own initiative, been able to impress their own boards with the necessity for intensive and expensive programs. However, acceptance of such expensive programs has often caused a transformation from a *social* agency into a rather highly specialized "clinic." In many areas today, instead of social agencies, we have adoption clinics, family counseling clinics, child guidance and similar clinics.

NEED FOR KNOWLEDGE

Another reason for inaction on social policy is the ignorance of the average social worker in a private casework agency as to how a community really functions. The art of politics, the interplay between the forces in any community's political situation, the process of getting legislation passed, all seem mysterious. There is general innocence concerning the power structure of communities, the manipulation of economic forces, identification of the key individuals in any community whose understanding of policy or program is almost tantamount to public acceptance. There is little to be observed in curricula that would promote better understanding of these phenomena. All the schools can do is to teach the social worker what to look for, but that would be a major step.

The day is past when social workers can simply camp on the doors of the rich until they get what they want. Today big labor, a key influence in many communities, is often as conservative a force as is big business. Where there is a close alliance between them, as in some federated fund-raising organizations, development of progressive social policy is a complicated problem indeed. Therefore, abdication by private agencies has not signified so much a lack of recognition of the social action function as a feeling of helplessness or inability to be truly effective in the development of sound social policy. As a consequence, many agencies have overlooked the fact that within their limited caseloads is the material that points up the need for social change and social action.

INACTION OF COMMUNITY PLANNING AGENCIES

The private agencies' need for help with development of social policy is further evinced by the failure of a great many private community organization structures to carry their responsibility for the major part of this function. Despite notable exceptions, community welfare councils or councils of social agencies have been markedly ineffective in spearheading social action.

I am not prepared to analyze why this is so, nor am I acquainted with the curricula of the major schools of community organization. I would, however, like to make some comments, based on observation of this situation. The close association of welfare councils with fundraising bodies—in many communities their absolute control be the latter—in itself reduces their effectiveness. Community Chest and United Fund boards are often dominated by interests reflecting the attitudes of the United States Chamber of Commerce and the National Association of Manufacturers—interests that are not reactionary in the basic sense of the word, but, at best, are not seeking ways by which expenditure of additional funds can improve social conditions. The highest-paid community organizer in the community is not infrequently identified with the very group that constitutes the greatest problem in changing social policies. Perhaps it can be better stated by saying that he not infrequently has lost his identification as a social worker.

There is also, it seems to me, an obsession with structure and reorganization of ·structure among welfare councils that keeps the community so constantly agitated that it has no time to look at unmet needs or the necessity for developing better social policies. This preoccupation has become so prevalent that recent reports of community surveys conducted by this country's major private community research organization have not commented on whether there were any unmet needs in the community. The rationale has been that, until the private agencies are reorganized, the community could not know but that they were spending sufficient money to meet all needs, and that increased efficiency, resulting from such reorganization, might be all the community needed.

In short, one needs only a quick look to see that there is a vast gulf between what private agencies recognize as sound social policy and what they are able to implement. Although it is true that casework agencies must become more effective in this area, it is also true that they are often subject to constraining forces outside their own structure. Despite these limitations, there is urgent need for self-examination and further development if they are to become even moderately effective.

THE SOCIAL CASEWORKER

The villains in this imperfect state of affairs are too easily viewed by many as the caseworker, casework training and casework philosophy. The dedication of the caseworker to save the world through therapy, case-by-case and person-to-person, is too readily, and perhaps unfairly, contrasted with the approach of the Kellys, Abbotts, Walds and others of yesteryear.

There can be no question but that the extensive amelioration of grossly bad economic and social conditions has justified turning our attention toward individuals. We have attained at least half a loaf of social welfare goals. Child labor has been almost wiped out in the United States. Imperfect as it is, public social policy does support a broad administration of public welfare. There are unemployment insurance, old-age and survivors' insurance, ADC, an enlightened philosophy of care of the mentally ill, a recognition that rugged individualism is incompatible with modern industrial civilization. We have made sufficient progress so that we can give attention to problems that cannot be solved by such broad measures—the interpersonal difficulties of parents and children, of husbands and wives, of the young and the aged.

Knowledge gained through social casework has contributed greatly to improvement and refinement of public welfare administration. I would also contend that training and experience in casework can be extremely valuable, if not essential, in the development of an individual's capacity for the sound implementation of social policy. In the first place, instead of a generalized desire to "do good," he is more likely to have a personal and real recognition of the need for social action. He is also more likely to recognize that any seeming solution for any problem will probably be a partial one. He will have more skepticism concerning his own generalizations, and, in his work with the individuals who are the essential tools in the development of sound social policy, the fundamental principles of casework will stand him in solid stead.

Training in social casework is probably not a sine qua non for the social worker who would make a career in social policy formulation, evaluation and implementation, but, in my opinion, it is an invaluable fundamental.

SOME PROBLEMS OF CASEWORKERS

Having straddled the answer, I would like to comment again on some of the present-day handicaps in the makeup of the social caseworker. Absorption of a vast body of knowledge about human personality, together with the never-ending development of skill, has served to confine many social caseworkers to the role of clinical technicians. As the pendulum in answering human difficulties has swung to interpersonal relationships, so has the caseworker's sense of "social" seemed to atrophy. For example, the social caseworker perhaps tends to discount the importance of good housing, as long as the people within it have unmet dependency needs or weak ego structures.

Social policy usually has to crystallize around a fairly simple and easily recognized concept. Caseworkers have had difficulty in enunciating these concepts. The existence of multiple causation of most human dysfunctions, the very fact that we are only at the beginning of understanding human beings, has created in many caseworkers a deep reluctance, if not inability, to generalize. It is perhaps no accident that most of the best interpreters of social casework to the general public are the administrators, the community organizers and others in noncasework positions. It may well be that their very ignorance of all the exceptions to the generalizations makes it possible for them to generalize.

One of the virtues of social casework and perhaps of social workers is also their undoing in affecting social policy. This is the workers' sense of integrity, their identification or overidentification with the people with whom they work, their conviction that they are right. Too often the social worker thinks himself alone in his compassion, his understanding and his resolve. He is too often extremely skeptical of what T. V. Smith has termed the "second-rate method"—the method of compromise. For example, in the development of standards of care—which are one expression or formulation of social policy—it is frequently very difficult for social workers to settle for anything less than perfection, for fear that in compromise they will have lost their integrity. Thus, because we know that the goal is really 10 feet away, we hesitate and often lose the opportunity to gain even 1 foot. I do not know whether this limitation is indigenous to social caseworkers or to human beings in general, but I do think it is more prevalent among caseworkers in private agencies than in most other areas.

There may also be something in the structure and practice within a private agency that isolates caseworkers from the practical realities of their community. The private agency, because it is not as responsible to the community as a whole as is the public agency, can more easily maintain certain discriminatory policies that sometimes result in ignorance of what is going on in the community. A public agency—if it is to survive—must recognize the pluralistic society in which it lives. It has to deal with the fact, for example, that there still exists in every community a sizable group of citizens who consider it morally harmful to assist adults who have failed. It has to recognize that there are sharp differences in viewpoint among various religious groups. Each day it is confronted with the validity of Lindeman's observation that perfection and democracy are incompatible (which could be paraphrased to state that perfectionism and effective formulation of social policy are incompatible). The private agency, if it so chooses, can pretty well isolate itself from differences, and the individual caseworker within the agency can become almost blinded to them.

The average social caseworker, it seems to me, lacks knowledge of the impact of religious differences upon the development of social policy. Child welfare is typically segmented into sectarian agencies; most "nonsectarian" agencies are essentially Protestant. I do not mean that the caseworker is oblivious to the fact that there are differences. However, his education is rarely broad enough to enable him to distinguish what is, for example, a matter based on faith, morals and dogma and what is simply the characteristic of a given development at a particular time, which can be questioned and changed if it is outmoded. In at least two or three states the issue of the religious care of children underlies a block that has balked the development of good child welfare legislation for a decade. Every social worker within those states, and in other states for that matter, should possess an extensive knowledge of the religious issues involved if he is to function in the field of social action. He must be able to identify what is tactic and what is an immovable basic.

For example, some who disagree with the position of the Catholic Church in respect to placement of children across religious lines wrongly identify other practices with which they are not in accord as official church positions. They may believe that the church stands behind the care of infants in institutions. There is no basic relationship between these two policies. Based on dogma, Roman Catholics are inalterably opposed to the placement of Roman Catholic children in non-Catholic families. This policy cannot be changed. It is a reality that must be accepted and respected. Alleged negative social effects of this policy can be overcome only to the extent of making certain that every Catholic child gets an opportunity for placement in a Catholic family.

That some Catholic institutions provide care for infants is a matter of tradition, not of religious dogma. Because of investment in buildings and the devotion of Catholic orders to providing this type of care, it is perhaps more difficult to effect a change than with other religious groups not so well equipped for care of infants. However, there is every reason to believe that, as the hazards of such practice are clearly demonstrated, trained casework staff becomes available, and money is found for foster home development, there will be as much movement to eradicate such care within Catholic agencies as in non-Catholic ones. In fact, in many communities this has already taken place.

GAPS IN SOCIAL WORK EDUCATION

There are many areas in which social work training is obviously deficient and where practice has not filled in the gaps. I have already mentioned lack of knowledge of community power structure and the process of obtaining legislation in a democracy. Other equally vital areas are understanding of the influence of federal, state and local tax structures on the ability of communities to provide services; and clarification of the relationship between government, tax-supported agencies and private agencies, the lack of which has increasingly led private agencies to seek public tax funds to buttress a financial structure weakened by ineffective solicitation of private funds.

There is need to recognize the social worker as an enabler, though not necessarily the activist, in the development of sound social policy. Essentially, social workers must work through community leaders; often they must develop them. Men like Marshall Field did not spring forth naturally with a concern and knowledge about children. They did not know intuitively what was sound social policy for children. In the background there was always a Sophie van Theis who devoted long hours to giving them knowledge and understanding of what was needed. Schlesinger's "Crisis of the Old Order"[1] aptly summarizes the influence of that type of social policy formulation on Wagner, the Roosevelts, Al Smith, Lehman and many others.

It seems to me that there may be something in the practice of social casework that causes a social worker to have a distaste for controversy, for conflict, for the joining of issues. Accepting in a social policy what may seem to be a radical departure from tested values often involves conflict and being at odds with at least a part of the community. And whether because of striving for prestige or simply the fact that social workers have families and personal needs of which Sophonisba Breckinridge might not exactly approve, the social worker today is inclined to be cautious.

In this area it is essential that the private agency be more courageous. The social worker in the public agency is unlikely to be as free as a private agency counterpart in expressing opinions, in lobbying for higher budgets, in taking unpopular stands. In spite of the efforts of some community chest boards to silence private agency employees, they have much more freedom to join in controversial issues than do public agency employees.

Much of the foregoing implies that, if social workers are to become effective in social policy formulation, this cannot be accomplished by simply adding a few courses to social work curriculum. Perhaps all we can suggest is that the generic training of all social workers be reexamined and that more attention be given to developing an attitude such that those who have the aptitude and interest will recognize their opportunities.

ROLES FOR THE CASEWORKER

Before leaving the specific subject of the caseworker, I suggest certain day-by-day activities for caseworkers that can aid in social policy formulation. One is to record and report conditions that cannot be remedied through casework as it exists, but that require changes in the policies of an agency or of a community, or the addition of new services. Such documentation can be concrete evidence absolutely essential to 1) the identification of need, and 2) the determination of how it can be met. Here it is essential to establish the mechanics whereby this material is brought to the attention of those within the agency responsible for action.

Another suggestion is that the individual caseworker be continuously alert to the opportunities for motivating people to act. For example, a caseworker in a children's agency recently received a telephone call from a physican bitterly complaining about the handling of one of his patients—a child in an ADC family who was being treated for an orthopedic defect. The doctor observed that the child was malnourished and very poorly dressed, and that the family was under severe financial strain. He had no difficulty finding medical resources for the child, but requested that the private children's agency do something to help the family. Instead of simply pointing out that the agency could not provide supplementary financial assistance for ADC families, the caseworker recognized a responsibility he had as a social worker. First he outlined briefly the extremely low ADC standards of the community. He pointed up the futility of attempting to ameliorate the conditions in one family when the same conditions existed in several hundred others in the community. When asked if he knew of other cases, the physician was able to recall two or three. When the doctor asked what could be done about it, the social worker inquired if other physicians in the community were observing the same thing. The doctor answered that he did remember two or three complaints. The social worker then suggested that the doctor get together with other physicians to find out how widespread the situation was, at least in terms of families known to private physicians. The doctor did precisely that. Eventually, out of the local medical society a committee was formed, with technical advice and assistance provided by a social worker. This resulted in an official representation of doctors protesting to public welfare authorities against the ADC standards, with several newspaper articles highlighting the bad conditions. Had this one caseworker believed that social action was the responsibility of somebody else, nothing would have been accomplished.

Caseworkers, when confronted with situations that are not properly within their function as employees of a private social agency, can function with their own professional organization or as private citizens. Kenneth Pray's observation that the individual caseworker functioning in a private agency cannot be free to take independent action as a staff member of an agency is a reality that must be respected. But it cannot excuse inaction.

The caseworker can also recognize that we are not talking about the large fundamental changes that have already been achieved. The caseworker cannot campaign for unemployment insurance. We have unemployment insurance. But he can be aware of the limitations of the present program, ways in which it can be improved, imperfections in its administration or its policies negatively affecting the individual. He can accept the responsibility of taking small steps, of making small changes. Altmeyer's observation that today one of the major areas of work in the development of better social policy is the perfecting of social reforms achieved in the 1920s and 1930s applies to almost the whole field of social work. One is always taken aback when a reporter asks, "What is the present-day program of your organization?" When you tell him it is essentially the same thing over which the organization has been striving for the last 20 years, you may feel ashamed. But the simple fact is that in a broad area of social policy, as distinguished from the perfection of techniques, essentially we have known for many years what has been needed. This applies to casework as well as to the Social Security program. We must look at new methods of dramatizing old problems, of ways of putting old wine into new bottles. As social workers, we should not be embarrassed in replowing old ground. The land may have been cleared and a few crops harvested, but there are still many rocks to dig out of the soil before full productivity can be reached. Digging out the rocks is perhaps not so glamorous as cutting down the trees; in fact, it's pretty grubby—but that happens to be where we are today.

Private social agencies must also learn that though it is good moral exercise, little is accomplished by simply issuing manifestos on broad issues. They must recognize the importance of reducing what they are attempting to achieve to specifics—to sometimes very small specifics; they must recognize that, as in politics, they must perfect the art of the possible.

THE ROLE OF THE PROFESSIONAL SOCIAL ADMINISTRATOR

Among the suggestions for future specialists in social policy formulation, there are several that could be applied in private social work. Large private agencies should have on the staff an individual responsible for that part of the agency's program involved in effecting social change. He might set up a fact-finding system through which caseworkers could identify and report remediable defects seen in their individual work. He could assist the administrator in work with the lay board and assist the lay board in work with the larger community. He could aid the sorely pressed staffs of councils of social agencies, where usually one person must carry this function for the total community. He could undertake the education of particularly promising board members who are likely to be in strategic positions to influence social policy.

This function is already being discharged in some private agencies where there are research personnel or where the administrator fortuitously sees this as a major part of his function and his board supports this view. For example, the executive of the Children's Home Society of California has had a tremendous influence—a background influence to be sure—in the clarification of many issues, with resultant radical changes in the child welfare programs in California. The executive of a small New England child welfare agency, taking to heart an admonition that ADC is also a private agency's responsibility, was directly responsible for a major change in the ADC program of his state. First, he educated his board, partly through case material brought to him by sensitized caseworkers; through the board he moved to the PTA, the Junior League, the American Legion and other organizations, and sparked an effective fire that caused an untrained, complacent public welfare commissioner to do an about-face in his attitude that all was right in that particular state.

Some statewide community welfare councils, such as the Michigan Welfare League and the Connecticut Child Welfare Association, have had important influence in developing sound social policy. Without question, the field of private social welfare needs to develop social-action vehicles that serve statewide areas, in view of the impossibility of meeting certain needs on a local basis only. There is ample evidence that, through the leadership of United Community Funds and Councils of America and other groups, there will be a continuing development of such statewide groups and organizations. The various forms of statewide child welfare social action groups developed around the White House Conference present another arena calling for trained persons. It is my hope that such groups will not be closely tied to fund-raising organizations. Certainly it is not possible to effect change without influencing those people who are going to pay for it, but it is best that the influencing be done after assessment of the problem, rather than that the influence come at a point where it will color the assessment.

The type of training required for the professional social administrator I leave to the wisdom of the educators. A greater emphasis on political science, economics, comparative religion and history is undoubtedly needed. And there can be no argument that a sound grounding in social casework is of major importance. How these essentials can be meshed and taught in the limited months a student is in the graduate school of social work, I do not know. Perhaps one area to be examined is the emphasis placed upon undergraduate training, particularly the preference existing in some schools for graduates from schools of sociology and psychology. History, political science and economics must have equal weighting in the preparation of the future social worker, if the heritage of the social reformer is not to be distilled from the blood of the social caseworker.

I add that encouragement should be given to the Council on Social Work Education's Committee on the History of Social Work. There are many social workers who learned of the proud history of their profession long after graduating from social work schools and then only because they read in other fields. If we suffer from a lack of the sense of dignity or importance or competence in social action, it is often because we are ignorant of our own history.

REFERENCES

1.   Arthur M. Schlesinger. Vol. 1 of *The Age of Roosevelt*. Boston: Houghton Mifflin, 1957.

THE ROLE OF THE PRIVATE SECTOR IN SECURING THE RIGHTS OF CHILDREN

It may be somewhat difficult for me to confine myself to discussing only the role of the private sector, inasmuch as the Child Welfare League of America, by which I am employed, is a membership organization embracing both governmentally supported agencies and privately supported agencies. I also believe strongly that the role of the private sector and the role of the public sector are reciprocal. One cannot do a good job without the other; they tend to sustain and support each other. Good private organizations are rarely found in communities where good public organizations do not exist, and vice versa. Low standards of service in the private sector tend to promote low standards in the public sector, and vice versa.

I also want to emphasize my belief that neither sector has an inherent superiority over the other. Each sector possesses some advantages in securing the rights of children that the other sector does not have.

My comments will deal primarily with child welfare services, which are designed specifically to ensure the child's right to care and protection. "Care is used broadly to mean providing or seeing that a child has whatever is considered essential for him to develop fully and to function effectively in society; in this sense, it also means fulfilling the child's right to these requirements. . . . A comprehensive system of child welfare services includes:

Prepared for the Rockefeller Foundation Conference on The Pursuit of Justice for the Child in Contemporary Society, New York, February 9, 1977.

a) Services to support and reinforce parental care
- social work service for children in their own homes
- child protective services for neglected, abused and exploited children
- services to unmarried parents

b) Services to supplement parental care or compensate for its inadequacies
- homemaker service for children
- day care service, both group and family day care, including services for children with special needs (such as emotionally disturbed and physically handicapped children)

c) Services to substitute in part or in whole for parental care
- foster family care service
- group home care service
- institutional care service
- residential treatment service
- adoption service

d) Preventive services
- social action to improve and ensure conditions and services that will promote wholesome child development, strengthen family life and preserve the child's own home; and to reduce the incidence of circumstances that deprive children of the requirements for their optimal development
- early case finding and intervention to protect children at risk and to avert unnecessary separation from their parents. . . ."[1]

THE HISTORIC ROLE OF THE PRIVATE SECTOR

The right of children to these services has been recognized to varying degrees. Historically, the private sector has played an extremely important role in securing the rights of children. Most of the child welfare services that we today consider essential for the protection of children were pioneered by the private sector—the establishment of orphanages to take the place of almhouses and indenture, the creation of a foster home system, the development of protective services for abused and neglected children, making adoption popular, the first provisions of day care. As in many other areas, most social reforms in child welfare were initiated by citizens banded together in private associations.

To act effectively, the individual citizen must have a means of gaining knowledge about the needs of children. Frequently his interest starts in a narrow focus or concern, as with his own religious or ethnic group, or with the children in his neighborhood. From such a foundation his knowledge increases and his aspiration to secure the rights of children broadens.

A classic example is the unlikely history of the American Legion's development as a major liberal force in lobbying for the creation of state departments of child welfare, the forerunners of state departments of public welfare in many states. Shortly after World War I, the American Legion set out to establish orphanages for the children of war veterans in every state of the Union. As they explored the needs of these children, they were persuaded by the Child Welfare League of America that institutional care of dependent children was outmoded, and were encouraged to think more broadly of children's needs. The Legion decided to fulfill its concern for veterans' orphans by attempting to secure the rights of all American children. It mounted a lobby that was responsible for the establishment of many state departments of child welfare. To this day, it continues to lobby for a broad spectrum of public and private child welfare services.

The California Children's Home Society, which originated out of the interest of six women in the plight of two children, developed into the largest private adoption agency in the United States, wholly supported by voluntary funds. In the 1950s it became the chief advocate for the development of public adoption services, convincing the California Legislature that adequate services for all children of the state could not be provided by the private sector alone. Hundreds of examples could be cited of the role of the private sector in obtaining recognition on the part of legislators in the public sector of the needs of children and the proper ways of meeting them.

Many other examples could be given of the way the private sector has demonstrated more effective means of securing the rights of children. For example, the Jewish Child Care Association of New York early recognized the deleterious effects on children of large congregate institutional care. In a relatively brief time it demonstrated that a 1000-bed institution could be reduced in population to a handful of children by effective child welfare services to return children to their own homes or to place them in small specialized institutions, foster family homes or group homes. This process was repeated many times across the country, particularly in the 1940s and 1950s, when the private sector was a prime mover in eliminating large congregate public institutions for dependent and neglected children.

Connie Maxwell, a Southern Baptist children's orphanage in South Carolina, demonstrated shortly after the turn of the century that it was more effective and humane, as well as less expensive, to provide a widowed mother with a cash allowance to enable her to keep her children at home than to bring the children into an institution. This innovative policy was the forerunner of the Mother's Pension movement and eventually the Aid to Dependent Children program.

The care and treatment of emotionally disturbed children were radically changed by the experimentation, in the 1930s, of two or three small private organizations which—against the advice of state departments of public welfare, the Child Welfare League of America, leading medical authorities and others—proved that children heretofore locked up in psychiatric wards, reformatories or schools for retarded could be successfully treated in an open community setting.

Interracial adoptions were pioneered by Louise Wise Services of New York, Children's Services of Connecticut, Children's Services of Cleveland, and a dozen other private organizations.

I could offer many more examples of experiments, innovations and "firsts" engineered by the private sector in securing the rights of children. Unfortunately, I could also offer many examples of lethargy, conservatism and resistance to change in the private sector.

RESPONSIBILITY OF PRIVATE AGENCIES AS ADVOCATES

The greatest importance of the private sector is not in the number of children it serves, but rather in its function as advocate of the needs and rights of children and as lobbyist for governmental action.

A few years ago this was forcibly brought home to me when a minister of welfare of an Iron Curtain country sought me out in Geneva. After making sure of the privacy and secrecy of the meeting he asked, "How do you create private child welfare agencies in your country?" His reason for wanting to know, he said, was that children's services in his country ranked last in budgetary priorities behind industry, the building of roads, services for the aged, etc. He had seen the usefulness in western countries of a lobby of private agencies to get more adequate governmental budgets. He wanted to know how private agencies came into being—how they could be established.

The need for private sector spokesmen, experienced in the provision of services for children, has been accentuated in recent years with the weakening of effective leadership on the governmental level. The merging of child welfare services into ever larger administrative units embracing health, education and welfare—both federally and locally—has been associated with declining governmental leadership on behalf of children, and declining appropriations.

For example, Title IV-B of the Social Security Act has been, historically, the most important provision for financing research, training and services for children. The authorization for this title is more than four times the appropriation, and the appropriation has remained essentially the same for 8 years.

Children have fared badly in revenue-sharing programs. They simply cannot compete with other interest groups who have a vote. The new Social Security title, Title XX, which in essence pits various categories of beneficiaries of social service funds against each other, demands well organized private interest groups if children are to receive their fair share of public funds. The more than 100,000 citizen board members of private child welfare agencies constitute a strong *potential* lobby on behalf of children's rights, providing these agencies do not lose their private characteristics and become wholly dependent upon government for their financing.

Today, the ability of the private sector in child welfare to serve as an advocate for children's rights is in grave danger. Alan Pifer has analyzed the situation in *The Nongovernmental Organization at Bay,* and *The Jeopardy of Private Institutions.*

The private sector has grown increasingly dependent upon public funds. The Child Welfare League of America found in a recent study that the proportion of their income that private child welfare agencies received from governmental sources rose from 28% in 1960 to 57% in 1975.[2] The decline in the proportion of private funding has been precipitous. The primary source of the voluntary dollar has been United Way-type organizations. Many are rapidly withdrawing from the funding of child welfare services on the basis that they are too expensive and that their funding is a governmental responsibility. If the proportion of governmental funds in the private sector continues to grow, we may reach a condition within the next 10 years in which it is likely that government will take over the operation of all private agencies, as it has in the provinces of British Columbia and Quebec.

A private agency that receives a high percentage of its funds from governmental sources is seriously compromised in its ability to be an advocate of children's services if that advocacy is opposed by government policy. Quasi-governmental agencies may have a positive role to play in service delivery, but I doubt very much that that role can be extended to effective advocacy. A major problem in coming years, therefore, will be how to avoid the demise of the private service delivery sector.

There is one part of the private sector that I believe should *not* be encouraged to develop, and that is the proprietary sector. Large and small business has recently been rapidly undertaking the provision of child welfare services. I am concerned primarily with the large business operation, not the "mom and pop" day care center or similar small operations. Business and industry may have a contribution to make to increased efficiency, but I suggest it is better and safer for business to make its contribution as consultants to the social service system, not as providers of social service. Businessmen can make a contribution, as they already do, by serving on the boards of voluntary agencies and in many other ways. But there is nothing in the record to recommend that we set voluntary nonprofit agencies and proprietary agencies in competition to see which can best secure the rights of children. We do not have the measures of effectiveness necessary to assure a fair test of efficiency and effectiveness between the proprietary and other providers of service. We do know, however, that the record of proprietary participation in the social welfare field is, for the most part, a record of waste and inefficiency as in the Job Corps, corruption and exploitation as in the nursing home field, and fast-buck artistry and standards evasion as in the proprietary day care field.

The president of U.S. Steel once said, "We are not in the business of making steel, we are in the business of making money." Making money is a poor bottom line for ensuring children's rights.

THE ROLE OF THE PRIVATE FOUNDATION

I agree with Dr. Henry Maier that "increasing the volume of services delivery will not be enough to overcome the effects of poverty." As he has pointed out, the critical issues are those concerning the development of adequate social policies that at least do not inhibit the implementation of programs. It is here that I think that private foundations can make a significant contribution. Private funding is needed in making sense out of a patchwork of programs; in improving the way in which care is organized and provided; in developing methods of quality control; in monitoring the effectiveness of the system; in building an advocacy network; in studying how to keep the public and private sectors in balance; in examining the implications of the entry of proprietary operations. It is precisely in these areas that governmental funding is likely to have serious limitations.

Finally, advocates for children cannot exist in a vacuum. There is need for people to monitor the system itself, but there is also need to help develop within the system the capacity for advocacy. For service delivery can provide the experience and knowledge underlying advocacy and can provide authenticity to that advocacy.

I do not, however, agree with the experts quoted by Dr. Maier that "without improved [family] income, no program of services can be enough to improve the conditions of children." Basic to the improvement of family life and thus children's life is, of course, the elimination of poverty. But waiting for the millenium does not excuse failure to invest in service delivery. Unfortunately, the eradication of poverty will not establish all children's rights or eliminate all children's needs.

REFERENCES

1. *A National Program for Comprehensive Child Welfare Services.* New York: Child Welfare League of America, 1971.
2. Barbara L. Haring. *Special Report on Funding of CWLA Voluntary Agency Members: 1960–1975.* New York: Child Welfare League of America Research Center, 1977, Table 1.

III.

CHILD
WELFARE
SERVICES

THE ROLE OF
THE MODERN
CHILDREN'S INSTITUTION

In this presentation I will pull together some of the general trends that we at the Child Welfare League see in children's institutions, and review the place that the modern institution has in the field of child care.

No field is changing more rapidly than institutional care of children. In the last 10 years particularly, there has been a tremendous surge forward in defining the place of the institution, and in reexamining its unique characteristics. More children are being helped as a result of our having identified the professional skills and competencies needed to carry out the job soundly.

FUZZINESS OF TERMINOLOGY

We are long since past the time when social workers argued whether institutions were necessary. I believe that everyone has shamefacedly given up the thought that foster homes could provide ideally for the care of all children. Whenever a social institution is going through a period of marked change, in this case a revolutionary change, there is bound to be confusion about definitions, and confusion and disagreement as to the precise function it should serve. Disagreement is useful because, as in any field of work with human beings, the extent and refinement of our knowledge are very small. We use words that convey some general idea, and therefore permit us to communicate, but if they are examined critically they do not contain precise meaning.

For example, one often hears the statement that every child in foster care is "emotionally disturbed." In a sense we mean that every child who is separated from his own parents is traumatized by that separation. But we have not identified by that term the degree or the substance of that disturbance. The very words "emotionally disturbed" form a cliché that has lost its exact meaning. When the lay public asks what we mean by emotionally disturbed—are there

Presented April 25, 1955.

degrees of disturbance? how do you identify them?—the best we can say is that there is mild disturbance, there is medium disturbance, and there is a serious disturbance. Some people, and I think this is good, like to think of emotional disturbance as constituting a spectrum without sharply defined differences in degree but rather with a gradual shading from children who have slight symptoms of unhappiness to children with symptoms of psychosis.

"Treatment" is another word that is being used universally in relation to the function of children's institutions, and yet, what does it mean? To some people its meaning is restricted to what takes place in an interview between the child and the social worker or psychiatrist. To others it means the group dynamics of the interaction of children and adults in the institutional setting. Still others, when they use the word, are thinking primarily of environmental manipulation. Obviously, the word itself can convey but a general thought. We have a long way to go before we can establish specific and clear definitions. I feel that much of the misunderstanding and differences of opinion that exist in respect to sound institutional care are based on our inability to communicate with each other because of the inexact words that we use.

It seems to me, however, that there is one common meeting ground for all of us: All of our thinking has to be based on a dynamic concept of human behavior. Whatever the discipline that constitutes our background, be it education, psychiatry, psychology, social work or group work, we see children as being the sum total of their biological and environmental inheritance; we place great importance upon the interaction of parent and child; and finally, we believe that human beings have tremendous resiliency, that they can change, that they can be helped.

Perhaps the most common dichotomy being used today with regard to children's institutions attempts to distinguish between what are called residential treatment centers for emotionally disturbed children and the traditional institutions. Many words have been expended in trying to define these two groups of institutions. We have to think of children's institutions not as being grouped into sharply divided categories, but rather as constituting a spectrum varying in their capacity to give effective treatment to children all the way from an institution that provides little but custodial care to one that treats the most highly disturbed children with the most highly evolved techniques, skills and concepts. When I use the words "treatment center" or "treatment-oriented institution," I am not thinking of distinct categories of institutions, for I recognize that there are subtle variances up and down the scale. Institutions at the two extremes vary widely in their professional orientation, and in their ability to contain and successfully help disturbed children.

BASIC ASSUMPTIONS ABOUT INSTITUTIONAL CARE

There are a few cardinal points to make. Whether these are called basic dicta or simply my prejudices I do not care, but I do want to convey something of my philosophy with respect to institutions.

1) Institutions are a vital tool in the complex of services that a community needs to serve children who have to be cared for outside their own homes. A rounded child welfare program is not complete without group care.

2) Our responsibility to children is to keep them as close to normal family and community life as possible. The most desirable place for the child is, of course, his own home. The foster home is the next most desirable situation, since it is closer to a normal family and community environment than is the institution. After these there is the institution, which serves many purposes for many children.

3) Even though a *bad* foster home is not better than a good institution, we must recognize that a *good* foster home is better than a good institution for the child and parents who can use it.

4) Many children are much better served by group care than by foster home care. In other words, the institution should be considered a specialized resource for children for whom a foster home is not suitable.

5) Institutional care is not a way of life. It should in essence be a means to an end, a means of restoring the child, who, for whatever reason, cannot live in a more normal community setting to the point where he can take his place there. To do this, institutions must have casework services as an integral part of their work. For every child who is out of his own home, there must be careful work with parents, and long-range planning. It is often when institutions do not have adequate casework service that children remain in care for many months or years after the necessity for that care has disappeared.

6) The number of disturbed children is increasing in the population of children's institutions, and will continue to increase.

7) I think that we have more than ample scientific proof that preschool children should not be cared for in institutions, or, to make it stronger, it is criminal for institutions to provide care for normal

preschool children. I think we are approaching the day when we will have laws—public health laws—forbidding this practice.

8) Finally, I do not think all institutions should become residential treatment centers. We have need for a wide variety of group settings—for shelter care, for detention, as group homes for adolescents, for observation. We need group care for temporary periods for children whose emotional ties to their own parents are so close or so distorted that they are unable to accept substitute parents even though their behavior would not prevent their living in a regular foster home. Another group of children for whom group care is usually indicated are those who, because of the deep rejection of their parents or a traumatic experience, have temporarily lost their ability to respond to the care of the average foster home. Then there are children whose lives have been so disorganized, so primitive, that they lack civilization, one might say; they have no manners, and are completely unfamiliar with the routine of normal living. Generally speaking, institutions are better able to accept the behavior of these children than are foster homes. Another group of children related to the first that I mentioned are children who'se own parents cannot accept foster parents and who need casework help to understand that foster parents will not take their children away from them. Finally, there are children from large family groups who, because of the shortage of foster homes that will accept four or five children in the same family, need group care until a suitable foster home can be located.

These are all valid types of care for the various kinds of children institutions can serve. Some of the children we have described could be labeled disturbed children, some could not. Why, then, has there been all of the emphasis recently upon emotional disturbance and institutional care? Why has the Child Welfare League for the last 4 years been studying residential treatment centers for disturbed children and trends in the care of disturbed children in traditional institutions? The reason is, as I have suggested, that the number of disturbed children in our institutional population has been increasing steadily and rapidly for the last decade or more. It is a trend that we believe will continue.

THE GROWING NUMBER OF DISTURBED
CHILDREN IN INSTITUTIONS

The most dramatic reason for this trend is the tremendous decline that has taken place in the maternal death rate in the United

States. Secondly, there has been great improvement in health standards generally. Parents are not dying early in life as they once did. In fact, the orphan has become a disappearing phenomenon in our society. This was graphically illustrated to me recently when I visited an institution in the South; in 1920 approximately 75% of the children in that institution were orphans; at the time of my recent visit, fewer than 8% were orphans. Nationally fewer than 3% of all children cared for outside their own homes are orphans.

Another major contributor to the decline of "normal children" in institutions has been the Social Security laws. Today 1,600,000 children in the United States live in their own homes with their parents or a surviving parent because of the ADC program. Twenty years ago thousands of these children would have been in institutions. General economic conditions have also improved so greatly that it is rare, particularly in northern states, to find children in institutional care for economic reasons. Church services, family services, child guidance clinics and comparable services directed toward keeping families intact have also done much to prevent unnecessary family breakup.

If a normal child must be cared for away from his home, he is unlikely to be referred to an institution, but rather placed in a foster home. So the institution, if you want to put it this way, is increasingly left with the disturbed or problem child who is not capable of living in a foster home. To put it positively, the institution, because it has been freed from the necessity of caring for large numbers of normal dependent children, can do the specialized job of helping troubled children regain their emotional health, develop the capacity to love and be loved, and take their place in their homes or in adoptive or foster homes.

I do not suggest that we are just discovering the problem child. Institutions have had problem children in their ranks for many decades. But I do think that for the first time we are becoming able to offer these children specialized programs and a pinpointed approach. When we speak of "problem children," we are simply talking about the rejected, the unwanted, the child who cannot say "thank you." Some of them are called delinquents, whom we do not want to send to training schools or penal institutions because they have not had a chance, and it is up to our institutions to give them a chance. Some of them are so unattractive and unloved that no one else will care for them. This is a tough job. It doesn't make for stars on the football team, or for nice shiny records that point up the number of graduates of the institution who have gone on to college or become vice presidents of banks. It is a job that, if faced squarely and embraced rather than resented, can produce tremendous results for our society.

INGREDIENTS OF GOOD INSTITUTIONAL CARE

When I speak of an institution I am not referring just to a place where a child lives while he is being given casework help or is being treated psychiatrically. The total institution is the treatment milieu. Casework and psychiatric help must be an integral part of the institution, but this is only one of the crucial ingredients of institutional care. Institutions have a unique opportunity to use the dynamics of group living as a positive force in the child's life. Institutions are able, if they know what they are doing, to provide an environment of low emotional pressure for the child who needs that. They are in a good position to prescribe the emotional, physical, spiritual, noncompetitive environment that each child needs. They have opportunities to observe unobtrusively and to bring a variety of resources to bear as the child needs them. No other form of foster care has all of these plus values.

Though the potential of these values exists in every institution, frequently they are not recognized or used. All of them are necessary if institutions are going to learn to work helpfully with disturbed children. The primary secret of an institution's superior ability to help disturbed children lies in the integration of all of the staff who are working with them. Institutions have to learn to cope with difficult children as their resources permit. It is very harmful for institutions to be pressed to take difficult children they cannot handle because they lack appropriate staff or funds. It is bad for the child and unfair to the institution. Rather, each institution must strive to increase the knowledge of its staff, add to its clinical resources, and reduce the physical demands made upon its staff in such a fashion that a personalized and specialized individual care can be given to each child. We need institutions offering a variety of resources. We need some institutions that are geared to work with children primarily through casework, with children who will be able to use ordinary public school and most community resources. We need other institutions that have a school in residence because they are working with children too disturbed to use public schools and other community resources. These institutions must have an intensive, total integration of staff. Another group are completely self-contained institutions that, because of the child's behavior difficulties and his lack of control, need to be closed, to have their own schools, intensive psychiatric casework help, and to have in particular, a staff that is living with the children, child care workers who are trained and skilled in understanding and working with disturbed children. And finally we need other closed institutions that will provide long-term care for children whose emotional problems are, like the cancer in the human body, problems for which we do not know the answers.

It is desirable for an institution to be a part of a multiservice agency that also has resources for working with children in their own homes, foster home care, homemaker service and other specialized forms of care that children in families need. The institution should not be in the position of accepting children after an investigation made by another organization, and releasing the children from care the moment they leave the doors of the institution. We must alter our modes of community planning and organization so that the institution becomes an integral part of the fabric of our social service structure.

All of us in the field of institutional care must clarify our own philosophy about such care before we can go forward. To me a basic tenet is the belief that institutional care is not a way of life, that in one sense the institution is like a hospital—a fine place to go when you need to be there but not a place to stay. Just as we are proud of our hospitals, we should be proud of our institutions. We can be proud of them without having to defend them as places where one would like to live for the next 15 years. We must gear ourselves to the concept of emotional nurture and not custodial care; to treatment, not simply retraining; to working with parents, not against them. We have to make sure that every aspect of our institution is designed for children and not for the adults who work there.

We have to become convinced that each person working with children is a professional without whose contribution our efforts are seriously impaired. If we can achieve this, our institutions can become truly centers for mental health, centers that prevent, as well as treat, problems.

Our job, in the last analysis, is to make certain that every child has the opportunity to develop to his or her full capacity. It is only as we break the vicious cycle of inadequate, disturbed parents rearing inadequate, disturbed children who in turn grow to become parents themselves, that we can ensure the mental health of our nation.

NEW KNOWLEDGE
AND NEW TRENDS
IN ADOPTION

There is no field of practice in social work to which the terms "new knowledge" and "new trends" are more appropriate than adoption. The field is changing so rapidly in the United States that before one study of practice is published, it has become outmoded. When I started out as a young caseworker in an adoption agency, we had to go out into the community searching for homes for children. I am not talking about homes for the older child or the handicapped child, but homes for healthy, normal, white infants. In the short span of 20 years adoption has become so popular and so socially desirable that agencies are besieged with many more adoptive applicants than there are babies available. This tremendous demand, which is in the main the creation of social agencies themselves, constitutes both a major problem and a major opportunity.

APPLICATION OF SCIENTIFIC FINDINGS

One reason for the rapidity of change is the recognition by adoption agencies, particularly within the last 5 to 8 years, that theirs is peculiarly an interdisciplinary practice. Not only are the social agency and the social worker involved in adoptions, but also the psychologist, the psychiatrist, the pediatrician, the lawyer, the geneticist, the anthropologist and many others. As research in those various fields has uncovered new answers concerning children, adoption agencies have used this new knowledge in improving their own practices.

Presented in Cleveland, 1955.

One application of new knowledge that has changed adoption practice in the last few years is the virtual discontinuance of delaying placement of babies so that their intelligence could be tested. Because psychologists had thought that infant tests could accurately predict potential intellectual development, agencies delayed placement for testing to ensure the child's going to adoptive parents of roughly similar capacity, and so to avoid the situation of adoptive parents with a very high intelligence adopting a child who could not possibly keep up with the family intellectually or educationally. However, relatively recent research has indicated that existing psychological tests for infants have little or no predictive value, though they do have value as one of several tools to judge a child's endowment. There is no longer any justification for holding children in order that they can be tested for intellectual capacity.

In 1954–55 the Child Welfare League of America studied adoption practices in 270 agencies. Fifty-five percent of these agencies considered the child's mental capacity an important factor in determining his placement, but only 30% of these still lag behind current scientific knowledge and hold children for a period of 2 to 6 months to give them a series of psychological tests to determine their adoptability. There is no question that the time is soon coming when, unless better infant testing methods are developed, no child will be held for this purpose alone.

Earlier placement has been the result not only of the findings in respect to psychological testing, but of the research that has been done all over the world showing the importance of consistent parental care of the child from earliest infancy. Conscious of the need of the parents as well as the need of the child of his or her being in a permanent home as early as possible, a few pioneering agencies have experimented with placing children in homes as early as the age of 2 weeks to a month, and have made careful studies of this practice. In many parts of the country the age of placement has been reduced by half over a 3-year period. Present scientific research places the child's ability to identify a specific mother figure at about 4 months of age, when the child first begins to have some visual identification of a caretaker. Movement from one mother to another can be more traumatic after that age than earlier. The consensus in good adoption practice today is that effort should be made to place a child as early as possible after relinquishment by the natural parents, and at least by 3 months of age. The only justifications for delay of placement are such severe emotional instability in the mother that she is likely to revoke a surrender, and medical findings that raise sufficiently serious doubts about the child's normality that further observation is necessary.

Another significant trend that has developed from both the scientific findings of other fields and the experience of adoption agencies is a great liberalization of the meaning of "adoptable." In League studies less than 7 years ago, many agencies questioned whether it was wise to place a child with physical defects or with limited intelligence; in short, they thought of giving adoptive parents only "perfect" babies and considered themselves responsible for giving a guarantee to parents for the future. Today the vast majority of agencies hold that any child is placeable for whom a family can be found, a family who, with full knowledge about the child, can and will accept him for what he is. None of the 270 agencies in our study admitted that a minor defect would deter them from placement, but a word of caution here is necessary. As in any field, there is often a lag between an agency's stated policy, the administrator's opinion, and what is carried out by the staff. We do know that there are still agencies that will not place children who have very low intelligence or have a family history of noninheritable disease, but here again the policy is rapidly disappearing, particularly as agencies are using the resources of geneticists and better trained physicians.

RELINQUISHMENT PRACTICES

The CWLA study of adoption practices uncovered certain undesirable practices of agencies, some of which result from unclear or unsound legal provisions or financial limitations.

Some of these practices concern the circumstances in which an agency will accept a relinquishment from the natural mother. A substantial number of agencies do not accept a final relinquishment from the mother unless it is clear that the child is adoptable, because they fear that, if the child is not adopted, the agency will be financially responsible for the child throughout childhood. What is needed, and fortunately exists in many states, is a policy on the part of the public agencies of accepting for placement any child who has been relinquished by his natural mother and proves to be unadoptable.

INADEQUATE SERVICES FOR THE UNMARRIED MOTHER

There is every evidence that lack of resources to care for the unmarried mother during her pregnancy is perhaps the most important factor in producing the gray and black markets in adoption. Few cities in the United States have completely adequate resources for the unmarried mother, resources that would enable her to obtain counseling help, financial assistance, shelter during her pregnancy, medical care and help in determining the best plan for herself and her child. In many of our large and wealthy cities there are but limited resources for financial assistance to unmarried mothers before delivery. A high percentage of unmarried mothers who relinquish their children in the gray and black markets are believed to do so to obtain adequate financial assistance and medical care during their pregnancy. A further detriment to good adoption practice in this area is a growing tendency among community chests of restricting agency service to mothers who are residents of the chest area.

AVAILABILITY OF HOMES FOR THE HARD-TO-PLACE

I would like to tell you at length about the rapidly expanding group interviewing of adoptive applicants that has so improved public relations of adoption agencies, but will confine myself to one important outcome of this practice. It was through this process that many agencies first discovered the willingness of adoptive applicants initially seeking an infant to consider adopting an older child or a handicapped child, after they learned how few infants were available. Out of the agencies' experience and a growing recognition of the opportunities that existed to find such homes, much has been done in the United States to find homes for these heretofore unplaceable children.

ADOPTABLE CHILDREN IN FOSTER CARE

The State of California has been the leader in finding adoptable children in foster care. A few years ago a group of social agencies organized the Citizens Adoption Committee of California. This group of over 600 citizens, with a strong component of doctors and lawyers, made an extensive study of adoption in their state, giving special attention to the problems of the older child, the handicapped child and the child of minority ethnicity. They studied the case of every child in foster care in Los Angeles, and found that 12% to 18% of the 3394 children in foster care needed "adoption planning," that is, could possibly have been placed for adoption. This finding startled the social work community, as it was the first documentation of the widely held impression that there were large numbers of older children in foster care throughout the country who should be placed for adoption. Following the study, Los Angeles adoption resources for older children multiplied many times, and the city now has the largest public adoption service in the United States. Recognition of the large number of minority-group children needing adoption placement—almost 40% of the total number were Mexican, black, Oriental or of mixed racial background—resulted in projects in San Francisco and Los Angeles in which a major effort is being made to find homes for minority-group children.

A recent New York City study indicated that 19% of all children in foster care in that city should have been or could be placed for adoption, were resources available.

What implications do these studies have for the field? There are 95,000 children in institutions and 145,000 in foster homes in the United States. If we use the most conservative figure of the Los Angeles study, 12%, it means that 28,800 children in the United States now in foster care could have been or should have been placed for adoption. That is a tremendous number of children. Perhaps Los Angeles and New York are atypical cities, but the correct figure for the nation is undoubtedly very large.

INADEQUACY OF ADOPTION AGENCY RESOURCES

If there are children in the United States for whom permanent homes could be found, we of course want to find them. But here we face a cruel dilemma. The critics of adoption agencies cry for the release of these children for adoption without facing what is required to free them. Most adoption agencies in the United States have sufficient resources only to place the infants who come to their attention. To do something about this problem of the older child, the handicapped child and the minority-group child who remain in foster care but should be placed for adoption, communities must have additional resources. Placing such children for adoption is no simple task. It is much more expensive than placing infants. It involves the most careful and continuous casework. It is absolutely necessary that two things go together—social agencies that are prepared to place these children and adoptive parents who want them. The League has had many opportunities to publicize nationally the availability of older children through TV, radio and national magazines. We continue to be concerned about the capacity and resources of many agencies to deal with the families who respond. This lack of resources creates a serious public relations problem for the social work field, not merely child welfare. There is no question in my mind that adoption agency practice is the most sensitive point of public relations between social work and the general public, if for no other reason than because it is the most widely publicized aspect of social work, at least at present. Every one of us must take a direct interest in this subject and do something about it.

Studies and facts are of no use unless they are accompanied by action. Professional social workers as such cannot produce that action without lay boards and interested citizens who can influence legislatures, chests, budget committees and the general public. We do have a tremendous opportunity to find at least 10,000 children permanent homes, and conversely, to find children for 10,000 waiting homes, but it is no easy task.

Today there is a movement sweeping the country to do something about placement of children with special needs. Agencies and adoption exchanges are beginning to prove that homes can be found. In selling to our communities the necessity for more adoption resources for the placement of these children, it is true that we can talk in terms of the emotional appeal of the waiting child, but we must not forget the economic appeal. The community spends the same amount in giving foster care to a child for 14 months as it would to place the child for adoption, and when a child is placed for adoption, the community expenditure largely ends.

The League estimates that it would be good economy if, for every 50 children in foster care in the United States, one adoption worker were available to review their cases and to find homes for those for whom adoption is appropriate. After a few years of such effort we could end the backlog of waiting children. I can think of no social service in the community that should receive a higher priority than finding permanent homes for homeless children. This is no little matter, and is one in which all of us engaged in social work have responsibility. These are children who cannot wait; if they are made to wait, the community will pay a heavy price in terms not only of the warped life of a child, but of the warped life of an adult.

In summary, there is a big job to do and it requires the concerted good will and effort of all of us to get it done. First, we have to make sure that agency practices are as efficient, as modern and as scientific as they possibly can be. This involves not only streamlining our own agency practices, but streamlining our community organization. For example, there is increasing evidence that services to unmarried mothers should be placed in one agency—all services, counseling, financial assistance, medical care, adoptive resources, foster home resources, etc. It is inexcusable to force the unmarried mother to go to a series of agencies to get the services she needs. Residence restrictions for unmarried mothers must be removed. We must publicize aggressively and openly the resources that exist to help unmarried mothers. Even in the cities that have the best record of agency adoption vs. nonagency adoption, only some unmarried mothers use adoption agencies; the rest go to the gray market and the black market. Only as we make adequate resources available to these mothers will they use agencies.

Second, we must try to obtain resources for the placement of older and minority-group children for adoption. Funds must be found for this purpose, and we must have both community chest money and public money. The job is too large for private philanthropy alone, but it cannot be done through tax funds alone either.

Third, as we get funds, we must publicize as widely as we can the fact that there are children other than infants available for adoption, and encourage people to apply for them. It is no easy task, but I think the families are there and are available. Fourth, we must equalize the opportunities for the minority-group child. Fifth, we must continue to make sure that the practice of adoption agencies reflects the best known scientific information, including the knowledge that has come out of our adoption agencies and that serves as the buttress of our practices.

UNIVERSAL DAY CARE: ITS MEANING AND PROSPECTS

In the history of the social welfare movement of the United States, the chapter covering the years between 1967 and 1972 will certainly have to reflect what might be called the "drive for universal day care." Although this drive is far from over, it is already possible to talk about the meaning of the movement and its prospects.

Day care has, of course, existed since the beginnings of the human race, and as an organized operation in the United States for more than 100 years. Until recently this service was regarded as a necessary evil, to be administered cautiously and sparingly only to those children who had to have it. Basic to this public caution was an almost universal belief that a mother's place—at least for the mother of young children—was in the home. An extensive day care study by the Child Welfare League of America made in 1968 found a public attitude that can be summed up as follows: "Mothers should not work; if they do work they are doing so for frivolous reasons; therefore, do not provide day care, for it will only further encourage them to do so."[1]

By the mid-1950s, however, it became apparent that whether or not the community provided day care, mothers in ever-expanding numbers were joining the labor force.

Gradually the social work establishment, which provided most of the organized day care in the United States, called for a change. Conferences convened by the U.S. Children's Bureau, the CWLA, the National Committee on Day Care of Children and others called for a major expansion of quality day care to meet the needs of working families and their children. The concept of casework

Presented at the National Conference on Social Welfare, Chicago, May 29, 1972.

screening as a precondition of obtaining day care was challenged and the concept of day care as a widely and freely available service for all children was advocated.

THE CHILD DEVELOPMENT MOVEMENT

A second historical force that has led to consideration of universal day care is the movement in the area loosely termed "child development." Its origins are in the nursery school and the kindergarten. Early-childhood educators have long seen day care as an opportunity to enrich the development of young children. Their interest was not in day care as a social institution for care of children, but as a setting in which nursery school programs that would stimulate the development of young children could be introduced. To oversimplify, the social workers' concern was to provide supplementary care of children—the educators' and psychologists' was to offer "child development."

It was this "child development" force that was behind the creation of the Head Start program. A task force of behavioral scientists, borrowing freely from social work in Israel and other European countries, conceived the highly popular program. Originally Head Start was administered as a part-time summer program. A later Presidential task force recommended that the programs, basically established to compensate for the developmental deficits of children from "disadvantaged families," double in brass as full 12-hour day care centers.

The "child development" expert recognizes the need for widely available day care, but frequently sees universal day care as a service around which can be organized child centers or parent-child centers that would embrace a wide range of services universally available to children whether or not they need full day care. The "child development" bill vetoed by the Adminstration was by no means wholly a day care bill—it was a broad child welfare bill embracing a wide range of services for children.

THE WORKING MOTHER

Many forces—often for very different and frequently conflicting reasons—are pushing for widely available day care. One such force, of course, is mothers working out of the home. The pressure of this force is obvious. The story of these millions of working women is a familiar one. There are millions of families who escape the label of welfare recipient because both parents work, regardless of the care available for their children. These families are caught in a cruel dilemma. If both parents work and they barely escape the welfare trap, their children suffer, but the children at least escape the socially undesirable situation of being on welfare. If a single parent decides that the children need her care, there is no alternative to welfare. And being on welfare is better only in one sense—children receive the care of their own parent.

Most working women who are mothers work out of economic necessity. That is true of both poor mothers and the so-called middle class mothers. If the work force currently is filled with millions of women who don't wish to work but have no choice, there is almost as large a pool of mothers who want to work but are not working because they lack decent day care. This pool of potential workers, and it includes a high percentage of the welfare recipients, according to one study, is another force, although unorganized, that pushes for universal day care. These women include many poor women who have decided that the care and supervision and love they can provide their children are more important than economic security or the small sense of pride at not being on welfare. These women include many skilled persons, at all economic levels, whose work is needed and whose contribution to the economy would be substantial. These women include those who require additional training or education prior to entering the work force, but whose children require care. These women also include those who, for whatever reasons, would prefer to work outside the home—whether for pay or as a volunteer—rather than working inside the home.

A group loudly clamoring for day care is labeled "Women's Lib." It is, of course, a composite made up of working mothers who would like to work, many women who are not mothers and many who will never be mothers.

Recently another group of mothers, more than 50,000 at this writing, has added to the pressure for day care. These are teen-age mothers, married and unmarried, who need day care for infants and toddlers if they are to continue their education.

Unknown until recent years are black and other minority group organizations that see day care as an opportunity, as the Black Child Development Institute interprets it, to demonstrate a child development center's capability to serve as a catalyst for community economic development.

A few employers want day care for their employees. Unions pursue day care as another bargaining objective that they may obtain for their members. College campuses have seen demonstrations demanding day care.

THE BUSINESSMEN FOR DAY CARE

A group whose influence is often underestimated is the day care businessmen. These persons, whether a part of the knowledge industry, the education industry, or spread through the broader social science industry, see day care, especially for young children, as a source of new business and of profits. The most ubiquitous are producers of materials, equipment and "information" who currently serve the traditional education "market." These businessmen are not interested in operating day care services so much as they are interested in selling the consumable supplies.

Another group of day care businessmen, which includes some of the supplies and equipment people, is actually interested in setting up and operating day care centers. Whether under the "chain" approach wherein they directly control operations with their own capital, or through the "franchise" or "joint venture" approach, where they indirectly control operations but utilize outside capital to a great extent, this group is attempting to expand its operations. It seeks the same sort of government-business relationship we have come to be familiar with from the defense industry. The relationship includes regulations designed to specifications of large, proprietary contractors. It features lobbying from a Washington office, something that community groups and voluntary groups are prohibited from doing. The relationship seeks the historical quid pro quo; private interests accept token regulation in return for guaranteed protection from real competition and, therefore, guaranteed profits.

Another group giving leadership toward obtaining universal day care is a coalition of legislators sponsoring various child development bills, including the one vetoed recently. Many of them are doing so out of their perception of the needs of families and children and the conviction that children deserve a higher priority in our nation's objectives. But many others doubtlessly recognize that the forces demanding day care include millions of voters.

"WELFARE REFORM" FORCE

However, I doubt that this discussion would be taking place at this time were it not for the most powerful of all of the forces interested in day care, namely, the force that moves under the banner of "welfare reform."

A tremendous portion of the current activity surrounding day care, including the activity in HEW and the day care industry, is in anticipation of passage of "welfare reform" day care—not comprehensive day care or universal day care. So, it is vital that we understand what welfare day care is for, and what it is likely to be. "Welfare reform" day care has but one purpose—to make it possible to get welfare mothers off the relief rolls.

Not so many years ago in the United States, it would have been unthinkable to propose that mothers be forced to place their children at 3 years of age in custodial day care centers of uncertain quality or in the homes of deprived, uneducated and overburdened welfare mothers, and take whatever job was offered to them.

The welfare reform day care push had first in mind reducing expenditures, and only secondarily—if at all—the welfare of children. All the groups that are a part of the universal day care movement must keep this in mind. Else, what they may be promoting may turn out to be a disaster for many of America's children.

The day care system the welfare reformists envision is one that costs the least amount of money and appears to meet the needs of those children most desperately in need of day care. Such a system operates at low cost only if administrative costs are kept to a minimum; hence, vouchers and income disregards are highly recommended. Such a system functions only if monitoring of quality and enforcement of licensing standards are token: hence, complaint systems replace monitoring and registration replaces licensing. Such a system is based on the premise that *any* care is better than no care; hence, custodial programs that offer relatively clean facilities and regular meals are considered real progress. Finally, such a system is based on a 19th century view of our society, when there were extended families, when delinquency and drugs were hardly the problem they are now, and when neighborhoods were supportive environments; actually, large portions of the population that should be receiving quality day care services, such as school-age children, are given minimal care or left to fend for themselves at too young an age.

The most likely prospect for day care today is, of course, "welfare reform" day care. It will be universal for one universe only—welfare mothers. Fortunately, the prospects for passage of welfare reform legislation get worse each passing day. The Administration's bad proposals have incredibly been made worse by the Senate Finance Committee and have almost no chance of passage.

Furthermore, the recent rapid expansion of day care under Title IV-A is likely to be greatly restricted in the future. The Administration has been greatly concerned that states were expanding day care to families other than those on relief under the clause of "past, present and future potential" welfare recipients. Twice it has asked Congress to "close the end" of the appropriation. Now, the Administration has announced that it will proceed to achieve the goal administratively. Although it is certain that the sponsors of broad child development legislation will continue to reintroduce such legislation, it seems improbable that such legislation can be passed over almost certain Presidential vetoes.

The short-range prospects of moving toward universal day care are rather dim. However, given the surprising size of the Congressional vote that passed the original child development bill, most observers believe that a major expansion of day care in the 1970s is highly probable. But such expansion will fall far short of universal day care—if we accept the term as meaning day care freely available to any parent who wishes to use it for her children.

DANGER OF RAPID EXPANSION

I, for one, am glad that the immediate prospects for universal day care are poor. To put it more strongly, if universal day care were to become available tomorrow, it would be a disaster for America's children.

First, it would inevitably be of low standard custodial quality. We have too many other priorities as a nation to expend funds for decent day care. Second, we have done too little experimentation to know what are the components of a good system of universal day care. We do not have the accepted standards or the enforcement know-how to prevent corrupt warehousing day care from driving out good day care. In addition to business, there are too many people who have a stake in day care whose major interest is other than the welfare of children. These include hundreds of newly ordained day care experts and consultants from several disciplines who see a lucrative career ahead; and the welfare reformers who see the welfare problem primarily in the form of black population increase and who, when they finally find out that providing day care is even more expensive than enabling mothers to care for their own children, will turn to some new panacea. I am dubious also about those who often have other agendas—community and economic development people, women's liberationists, etc.—whose main concern is not always the welfare of the child.

One of the most critical issues in providing day care—community or parent control—has not been resolved. There is much evidence that in a pluralistic nation like ours, with this imperfect state of the art of designing day care programs, meaningful parent participation may be a crucial variable in programming beneficial day care.

I am also afraid that, if universal day care were to become available quickly, we would fail to reexamine the proposition that it is in the infant's interest to enable every mother to have a genuine choice as to whether she works outside the home or not. In my view, mothers of young children should be paid an adequate "wage" to stay at home and care for their children. I would want freely available day care only after we had guaranteed mothers a real choice.

There is also insufficient evidence about many aspects of day care. For instance, that it is possible to provide widespread programs of day care that are not harmful for children under 3 is questionable—in spite of recent enthusiasm from child development researchers. It is a long way from an ideal, high cost laboratory experiment to a universal provision of such care.

What type of training do we need for day care personnel? What type of person can do the best job as defined by age, education, ethnicity, sex, etc.? Who should administer day care centers—the public/private business interests?

In a rapidly changing culture, what would be the effect of universally available day care on family life? Such universal day care implies that any mother, for any reason, can place her child in a day care center for whatever number of hours she wishes. What would be the effect of such provisions? Would some restrictions prove necessary to protect children, or would parent education prevent abuse?

Many other pertinent questions can be raised about our readiness to commit ourselves to universally established day care. The important thing is that the issues be raised and then carefully examined through demonstration and research. I want to make it clear that I am for expanded, high quality day care. I am for much larger appropriations for model day care agencies, for demonstrations and for assistance to the millions of mothers who need day care now. But unless that day care is of such a quality that it enriches the child's life, it is to be opposed.

ROLE OF THE CHILD ADVOCATES

The final force is the one I shall speak the least about because it is the force that includes, in my opinion, groups such as the Child Welfare League of America and, I assume, includes all of you. That force, which I call the child advocates, believes that it is interested in a universal day care system because such a system is needed by children and parents. This group has been leading the fight for *quality* day care, for standards similar or superior to those outlined in the *1968 Federal Requirements*, and for a commitment of funds sufficient to deliver such day care services to all children who need them.

The child advocates, as the name implies, have as their point of departure the needs of children, first and foremost. Needs of parents are also considered, but this is a secondary consideration. And the other needs outlined, such as the need to reduce welfare rolls, to reduce public expenditures, to liberate women, are of relatively little importance.

The child advocates see their role as one that involves no self-interest. In many ways, we represent an idealistic point of view, and therefore expect that our positions will not be the decisions adopted by public policy makers as a result of political processes involved in compromising. Nonetheless, we stick to our principles. We believe that it is critical that the rights and needs of children be represented unwaveringly; we know that compromises will be made, but we do not approve of them.

While we will accept the label "idealist," we also claim the label "ultimate pragmatist." There is nothing so practical as realizing that cut-rate solutions will not work when drastic, essential changes are required. For this reason, of the forces crying for universal day care, it is probably the voice of the child advocates that keeps insisting on inserting the word "quality." We do believe that anything less than universal *quality* day care is counterproductive, and that is what we will continue to insist upon, no matter how impractical, over the short view, we may seem to be.

REFERENCES

1. Florence A. Ruderman. *Child Care and the Working Mother: A Study of Arrangements Made for Daytime Care of Children.* New York: Child Welfare League of America, 1968.

THE RESPONSIBILITY OF FAMILY AND CHILDREN'S AGENCIES FOR REHABILITATION OF FAMILIES

Particularly during the last 10 years, the differences between family agencies and children's agencies have become less and less. Although family and children's agencies have different focuses, both are set up essentially to work with families with problems and, it is hoped, the treatment the family will receive will be basically the same. But the question of the differences and likenesses in the responsibilities of agencies for rehabilitating families cannot really be tackled through any simple shifting of agency location or structure. Meeting the problems requires great thought, plus the overcoming of an immense overlay of meaningless slogans and pious hopes we so often express. I suspect that in some ways we have a more difficult situation in our field today than we had some years ago, when significant differences between family agencies and children's agencies were more important.

I have been asked to talk about the theoretical considerations of strengthening family life. Although differences in practical application still exist in the field, there are few, if any, theoretical differences between family and children's agencies when it comes to recognition of the necessity of viewing the family as a whole, of viewing work with the child only in the framework of the family. The "family-centered" philosophy, however, is only a philosophy, the meaning of

Presented at the Family and Child Welfare Conference, Community Council of Greater New York, Carnegie Endowment Building, March 14, 1961.

which is sometimes difficult to ascertain when one looks at practice. Though we may have no theoretical differences, I think it clear that there are sharp differences in practice and in approach.

One rich area for research, both on an intensive level and on a superficial one, involves looking at statistics for clues as to wherein differences lie. There is a rich area for the examination of practices in public and private agencies, and in child guidance clinics, which I have added to the list because here again are apparent sharp differences in respect to treatment of children. An example of such differences is found in a statistical examination of the percentage of unmarried mothers who release children for adoption among those seen first by family agencies and those seen first by children's agencies. In general, a much higher percentage of mothers releasing their children have first gone to a child welfare agency, rather than a family agency. Another area in which there are probably sharp percentage variations is in child placement, as it pertains to whether the family has first gone to a child guidance clinic, to a family agency or another agency not having placement facilities, in contrast to the family's going to an agency that has placement facilities. These differences should not exist if there were really a common base of practice, of theory and of knowledge of the implications for the mother and child dependent on a particular decision. Beyond question agencies' particular biases or convictions affect how we work with families, whether or not we are aware of them.

FEASIBILITY OF REHABILITATION

Our feeling of responsibility for strengthening family life often causes great guilt on the part of agencies. We are all certain that families can be rehabilitated. Sometimes I think, however, that we assume guilt unnecessarily when we fail. Some agencies simply do not have the skills or personnel to do effective work. They probably should not be permitted to exist. It is a fact that most children's agencies in the United States lack either the facilities, the know-how or the trained personnel to do anything approaching effective rehabilitation work with families. When I say most, I am talking about some 1800 private agencies and some 2000 public agencies in the country that could be classified as children's agencies. Fewer than one-quarter of these agencies even have caseworkers! There are others, well equipped, who still seem to fail.

As an example of an agency's assuming unwarranted guilt, I recall one of the best agencies in the country, outstanding in its treatment services for disturbed children. Extremely concerned because parents of very few of the most difficult children under care and treatment were actually involved in anything resembling an intensive treatment relationship, the agency had conducted a case-by-case survey. The conclusion was that the word "family" was completely inapplicable to most of the parents involved. In most of the cases, no "family" had even existed. Two disturbed adults had simply produced a child; they had never produced a family nor, within the limits of present scientific knowledge, was it possible for anyone to enable them to do so.

What do we mean when we talk about "the family?" To me, the family exists when it is an organism able to nourish children effectively. That is the basic purpose of the family. There are many adults who have children, but not all adults with children can be called families. We should not heap coals on our heads for not being able effectively to rehabilitate a nonexistent family, nor should we take the easy escape of giving up on all families. Most of my emphasis is on our failure to provide effective help to the families of children in care in the United States.

INADEQUACY OF REHABILITATIVE EFFORTS

A national study was made recently for the Child Welfare League by Dr. Henry Maas of a cross-section of children in foster care in this country. The results were shocking. Many of you are familiar with the study, but I quote just one or two statistics as evidence of our failure (for whatever reason) to make certain that when a child is removed from his own home, real efforts are made to find some permanent way of life for him, instead of simply letting him stay on indefinitely in a limbo of foster care. We in the United States have been deluding ourselves that foster care is a temporary way of life for children. This is not true. If a child is in foster care for 18 months or more, he is likely to be in care for the rest of his childhood. And, for at least a quarter of the children in care in the United States, long-term foster care is indicated, since it is not possible for them to be placed for adoption, nor can their families be rehabilitated because the situations are too deteriorated.

In this study involving a typical cross-section of children in foster care, it was found that parents in one-half of the cases had not visited their children for at least a year. These were parents who could have visited had they cared to, since parents in prison or in mental hospitals were excluded from this statistic. An examination of the parent/agency relationship revealed that in fewer than 20% of the cases was there anything remotely resembling an effective relationship. Ineffectual and haphazard work with parents characterized many of these cases.

These statistics alone, I think, show the seriousness of the problem we face in attempting to rehabilitate families. On the one hand we should not delude ourselves into believing that simply because we have the shibboleth of strengthening family life, all families can be so strengthened and put back together, and therefore good foster care services are unnecessary. On the other hand, we should not kid ourselves into believing that in any part of the country there is anything even approaching effective work with the whole family of those children with whom we are concerned.

There are, of course, some serious practical limitations when we approach this problem. Regardless of our desire to work together effectively, when we do not have certain major tools to keep children in families, we have to make an overuse of foster care. I am referring specifically to the gross underdevelopment of such services as homemaker services and effective day care, including foster family day care. Lack of such facilities makes it more difficult to avoid the precipitate decisions that so often characterize our work with children and result in parents' becoming completely divorced from their children. This haste is also caused, in part, by the very human reaction that motivates most of us—when we see a very bad family situation, we feel impelled to move in quickly, instead of realizing that there are few real emergencies. Emergency cases involving seriously disturbed parents do demand immediate attention. But probably as many as four-fifths of the so-called emergency placements of children are entirely unnecessary. In these cases, the actual or potential harm that might be done a child by leaving him in an admittedly bad situation is much less than the potential harm of removing him precipitously. We usually fail to obtain an accurate understanding of the family's dynamics and its relationship to the community, which would help in determining whether or not some plan short of removing the child would be more effective.

MISGUIDED AGENCY POLICY

Many agency policies accomplish precisely the opposite of what is intended. To cite an example of certain simple questions of policy that sharply affect our work with children: A family in a nearby suburban community, able to pay for foster care, sought placement for a child. No agencies in this New York suburb accept children of families able to pay for the cost of care. The family tried advertising, and received replies from a large number of licensed foster parents. This aroused my curiosity, since agency foster homes were very scarce. Why did these persons respond to a private ad when the amount offered was no greater than that offered by the agencies?

One woman of limited education, aged 55 or 60, speaking in rather broken English, explained the situation. She felt that the agencies' policies governing parents' visiting, particularly in the initial and crucial stages of the child's placement, were, in effect, permanently separating families. The agencies for which she had boarded children did not permit parental visits during the first month of placement, presumably to "make things easier" for the child and foster parent. She finally said that the only way children can assimilate and understand what is happening to them and learn to live with it, is to *experience* it. Though it is difficult to have a homesick, troubled child on one's hands during the first month, the child is more likely to make a much better adjustment than if he is simply forced to suppress his grief and fears about being separated from his parents. This simple illustration points up how agencies can set up routinely applied policies that have the effect of separating parents from their children or children from their parents, as well as alienating potential foster parents.

Not infrequently agencies without their own placement services have such an idealized view of what can be achieved through placement that they may regard foster family care or types of institutional care as far better than they are. They lack sufficient understanding of what placement does to children separated from parents, or how to work with the separation anxiety that every child experiences in these situations.

On the other side of the coin, agencies frequently consider placement of a child in foster care as essentially a failure of family casework. A child is placed in foster care only when a situation has become so aggravated that he has been severely damaged. Somewhere in between, of course, is where we need to be. Despite what

I have said about the harm that can be done when children stay on needlessly in foster care, foster care can be an extremely positive, growth-developing experience for many children and, as such, is a vitally needed service.

DIFFERENCES IN PERSPECTIVE

Although the theoretical concepts of family agencies and children's agencies may sometimes be the same, actual experience may cause them to work differently. I cite a recent experience. It involved an interagency disagreement over the necessity for certain types of treatment facilities for children. A family agency saw no necessity for placing a group of 40 to 50 children in a treatment center operated by another agency. It testified that, in its experience, almost all the children could be treated on a noninstitutional or outpatient basis. In this same community, another residential treatment center for children had recently hired a new executive who had just left a 15-year job as executive of a large family agency. When his opinion was asked, he said that it was the most disturbed group of youngsters he had ever seen. I was curious and asked him for an explanation of the difference in viewpoint. His answer was that most of the children in the treatment institutions never came to the attention of family agencies in that city. Families showing severe neglect of children, in his opinion, rarely walked into a child guidance clinic or family agency.

We frequently see things from different vantage points, forgetting that our own experiences are not always rounded ones, despite the similarity in our theoretical viewpoints. One purpose of this conference is to bring us up to date on what is happening in other fields that we can apply to our own. In our field we face dangerous isolations. Sometimes it is physical isolation, where our placement facilities, far from the city, make effective work with families practically impossible. Also, we have not developed working relationships with other agencies that permit effective work with families. There is nothing more dangerous to our clients than this lack of communication among agencies, though its solution is not simple. A multifunctional agency can be just as divided and isolated in its programs as separate agencies.

Essentially, our problems cannot be solved by structural manipulation alone. They can be solved only by making sure that every agency, regardless of its name and title, has the tools to work with and the range of services required for effective operation. We must make sure that every agency makes a major investment in communication, enabling it to work effectively on a common basis of understanding, subordinating its identity within a community network of services. We must make certain that all agencies are aware of their severe limitations; none of us has a monopoly on knowledge. We must be aware of what we are supposed to be doing and be willing to face the fact that the work we do may be aggravating the family's situation.

I hope that this conference is simply the beginning of an extensive examination of agency relationships that will contribute to the development of a common approach to families and children.

IV.

EDUCATION
AND UTILIZATION
OF STAFF

PERSONNEL NEEDS

There is no possibility of providing master's level workers for every job in the child welfare field that we so often think requires an M.S.W. worker, and it is a serious question whether M.S.W. workers are needed in many of these jobs. Not facing this reality can injure thousands of children and families. What are some of the roadblocks that prevent or delay resolution of this problem? Let me briefly list some of them that have been pointed out by many observers.

FAILURE TO FACE FACTS

One is the lack of communication within an agency, between agencies, and between agencies and the graduate schools of social work. As a field, we have not got together and realistically faced the blunt facts. More than the public agencies, the private agencies have not faced the facts, for they are protected by a closed intake and can cut their programs to suit the numbers and training of their workers. The public agencies have not been able to do so—they must serve all children who come to them. However, they have frequently carried an air of false shame because they had so few M.S.W. workers, instead of facing how they could best utilize staff members who were available.

RIGIDITY

Rigidity in supervision and administration, impossible "standards" and the insistence on carrying out tasks in ways that have become hallowed with age, rather than analyzed by careful study, are other roadblocks. The overprotective attitude toward the worker-client relationship, surrounded by a mystique that can be penetrated only through the magic of 2 years in a graduate school of social work, has been a major detriment. Professional bias has blocked efforts to

Presented in February 1966.

develop and utilize the assets of the nonprofessional. And, as has been pointed out many times, this is a characteristic of a young and insecure profession.

PROJECTION OF RESPONSIBILITY

Too many agency boards and executives regard the supplying of personnel as somebody else's responsibility. It is the responsibility of the school, the government, or anybody but the agencies themselves. This is reflected in rigid attitudes toward the number of students that the agency can train, insistence upon the second-year student, refusal to provide scholarship money, and a supercilious attitude toward agencies that do not have M.S.W. personnel. Thus we find well financed private agencies in towns where there are three graduate schools of social work and where the salaries are 20% above those elsewhere assuming that it is because of their excellence that they have all M.S.W. workers. "If only all other agencies were as excellent, they would all get M.S.W. workers."

To be fair, the fact is that top-level staff are so overburdened, so consumed with the pressure of daily work, that they frequently have small chance to look at the broader picture and to realize what their profession as a whole must examine.

AMBIVALENCE TOWARD THE NONPROFESSIONAL

The last roadblock I mention is simply our deep ambivalence toward the "untrained." We know we have to use persons other than the 2-year graduate, but we really don't want to. We state that they can do as effective a job in some areas and perhaps an even more effective job than M.S.W. workers, but we really don't believe it. We give speeches about the great usefulness of volunteers but we really want some other agency to use the volunteers. It is not a pretty picture.

A major result of our attitude toward the use of personnel has been an overemphasis on quality of service at the expense of quantity. This plays into the tendency to consider the problem one of quantity *versus* quality, rather than of quantity *and* quality. Furthermore, our exclusive reliance on a professional staff of graduate workers has not necessarily resulted in any provable, significant increase in quality of service.

By devoting primary attention to the professionally well equipped service, we have tended to minimize the necessity of raising the standards of less well equipped but equally vital services. This position has tended to limit professional responsibility for developing programs to meet social need to those that can be professionally staffed and those that fall clearly within the casework method. Undoubtedly, the overemphasis on casework and the training of graduate social workers in the last 30 years has accentuated all of these difficulties.

Perhaps the most serious and destructive result of our overemphasis upon training and the percentage of trained staff in any particular agency is the splintering of the social work profession that has resulted. We have severe "prestige" difficulties in social work, and we have, perhaps not deliberately but nevertheless successfully, developed a pecking order of prestige that has little or no relationship to priority need for services. This has seriously skewed the attitude of one set of agencies toward another. The ironic aspect of this situation is that it is primarily the product of what training funds were available, rather than of any recognizable virtue.

The pecking order goes something like this: Because the so-called psychiatric agencies have the highest percentage of graduate social workers, the psychiatric social worker looks down upon those employed in family agencies, who come next in the scale. The family agencies in turn look down upon the child welfare agencies and their workers. The social workers employed by the private child welfare agencies are able to look down upon those employed in the public child welfare agencies because they have a much lower percentage of M.S.W. workers. The public child welfare agencies are able to look down upon the public assistance departments, which are at the bottom of the heap, with only 3% or 4% M.S.W. workers. The false prestige that has been attached to working in the agency with the highest percentage of graduate workers has resulted in a blind, irrational preference of workers to be employed in the highest prestige service without any regard to the importance of the service or the need for it.

Bitter hostilities have developed between various functional agencies, in large part because of these "looking-down-the-nose" attitudes. For example, I believe that the low priority that many public assistance administrators attach to child welfare today is in large part the result of years of child welfare workers' contemptuousness of their public assistance colleagues. The push to integrate and merge services has its base in part at least in precisely the same situation.

DIFFICULTY OF PROTECTING PROFESSIONAL STANDARDS

Another factor that has delayed our grappling with the problem is the fact that over the last 30 or 40 years, social work has often been involved in a major struggle with lay people, with civil service examiners, and with budget committees to get them to recognize the necessity of employing M.S.W. personnel. If, at the same time, it were acknowledged that persons with lesser training could work adequately at some jobs, the professionals were afraid that they would never get recognition of the necessity for M.S.W. workers in most jobs. Years of reading newspaper reports critical of what "social workers" did or did not do, reports that in most instances referred to persons without either social work training or social work orientation, added to the reluctance to recognize any but the M.S.W. worker. Although the term "social worker" in the popular press and magazines and in legislatures has in recent years increasingly denoted a trained professional, the fact that the general community has a poor understanding of what "social worker" means has also reinforced our ambivalence toward the "untrained" and the volunteer.

Fisher observed: "Happily, the divergent views have been modified in recent years. There is a growing recognition that while some jobs in welfare do require full professional competence, there are many that could be effectively carried by people with lesser qualifications."[1]

Although progress has been made, there is still a hard core of resisters to be found in agencies and in schools of social work. Witte observed: "There are those who believe that we should not disturb present developments. They are pleased with the improving status which social work is achieving, with the improvement in the established standards, and they fear that any plan which deviates from the present educational pattern, however worthy its purpose, is a threat to those hard-won professional standards."[2]

It must be admitted that national standard-setting agencies such as the Child Welfare League of America have aided and abetted this stance. For example, most standard-setting agencies place a premium on having fully trained staff, or at least they have developed formulas that establish a minimum ratio of trained to untrained staff members. It would be far more sensible were the national agencies to develop standards that establish not only a minimum but a maximum ratio of trained to untrained staff. Such a national agency would not only refuse to accredit the agency of poor personnel standards, but would refuse to accredit an agency that was overutilizing or poorly utilizing trained personnel.

PROMISING DEVELOPMENTS

There is, of course, a brighter side to this picture. There are many agencies that are trying to reach a balance. For the most part, it is public agencies that are in the forefront, since they have been forced far longer than private agencies to recognize the personnel reality. Many agencies are striving hard to find tasks previously "reserved" for the professional that can be done as adequately by the volunteer or nonprofessional. They no longer think simply of chores like chauffeuring, supervision of infants during clinic visits and stuffing envelopes, but are identifying substantive jobs that can be done as well or better by the nonprofessional.

Many public agencies are primarily manning supervisory and executive jobs with professionals and using as much of the time of these people as possible for on-the-job staff development. Schools of social work have developed short-term courses, summer schools, night schools and extension courses. Agencies are participating in workshops, institutes and conferences that are specifically aimed at recruitment and inservice training of the nonprofessional. Although many agencies have recruited the nonprofessional in anticipation that he will later go on to professional education, in fact at times making this a requirement, other agencies are recruiting staff for whom professional education is not anticipated but for whom the agency will provide inservice training. The emphasis in this type of approach is on the compatibility of the worker's interest and potential skill with the assignments that he is given. Some agencies are experimenting with a team approach—the handling of caseloads by a team headed by a professionally trained worker but fully utilizing the services of one or more nonprofessionals. Others have developed intensive training for volunteers. These and the myriad other experiments that are being carried on constitute a big step forward.

Another beneficial effect of the personnel problems has been the fact that casework agencies are looking more favorably on techniques other than the one-to-one casework interview, and giving increasing emphasis to group services, such as group meetings for information and educational purposes, group therapeutic methods, and group sessions at intake with foster parents, with parents of children, with adoptive applicants and with unmarried parents. Agencies have also been willing to employ part-time staff, and all have intensified efforts to "sell" social work as an attractive, rewarding field. Basic progress has been made in examining those tasks that the nontrained person can do as well as or even better than the professional. The emphasis upon "indigenous" personnel has as its base that concept. Agencies have found the most effective foster home recruiters are foster mothers themselves. They have not only discovered a way to relieve the demand for professional personnel, but have found that the nonprofessional can often be more effective than the professional.

REFERENCES

1. Philip S. Fisher. "A Look at Social Work Training." *Canadian Welfare* (November/December 1964).
2. Ernest F. Witte. "Training Social Welfare Aides." CSWE Annual Program Meeting, January 24, 1963.

EDUCATIONAL EXPERIENCE AND PRACTICE DEMANDS

Underlying any discussion of the articulation between educational experience and practice demands is the fact that we are only partly able to identify which practice we are talking about and which educational experience we are discussing. In spite of many attempts, no definition of the profession of social work has really succeeded in identifying it in such a way that it can be clearly perceived by those outside of the profession—or inside it, for that matter.

DEFINITION OF SOCIAL WORK

The Council on Social Work Education defines social work as "a profession that is concerned with the restoration, maintenance and enhancement of social functioning."[1] Two dozen other definitions could be quoted, and we would still end up with a definition so broad, with other limits so ill defined, that only rough communication is achieved.

The primary onus for making a clear and useful definition rests with the graduate schools of social work. The practitioner in his agency setting does not have to be quite so concerned, and he is not. He is usually engaged in or administering a specific service, such as public assistance, marital counseling, services to the aged. Under the general rubric of social work, he is performing a defined task that is easily understood by himself and those around him. It is to be hoped that he brings to his job a professional discipline, an awareness that what he is doing lies within a much larger framework of efforts to produce a society that functions successfully.

Many practicing social workers equate "social work" with their specialization. They cannot tell you what is generic about their jobs

Presented at the Annual Program Meeting, Council on Social Work Education, Salt Lake City, Utah, January 24, 1967.

and the jobs of others who are also called social workers. For social work practice is specific, not generic. An agency's concept of what social work education should be is often understandably "egocentric"—related to its own particular function.

The task that social work educators have in attempting to define social work and to educate for it is one for which I have the greatest respect. Considering the complexity of merely identifying the professional discipline of social work, it is little wonder that determining what education is necessary to produce the professional worker equipped to work in a myriad of practice settings is extremely difficult. The job would be hard enough if the scope of the profession were relatively static, if the practice of social work were at least reasonably fixed. At a time when practice is undergoing major change, it is not surprising that practice and education are sometimes out of joint. As John Gardner has pointed out, not only are the "familiar ways of doing things . . . becoming obsolete," but it may well be, as he indicated, that within the next 30 years the school of social work may be known by some other name.[2]

Within social work education there are many conflicting ideas as to what social work is. At a time of so much pull and haul, so much lack of fit between one idea and another, it is understandable that there be some sharply conflicting views as to what we are and where we are going or should be going. This was demonstrated in an article on social work that appeared in *Mademoiselle* magazine.[3] This article, which presented an essentially negative and confused view of social work as a potential profession of choice for college graduates, was in part the product of confusion within education itself. It was apparent that the writer, in interviewing faculty members of graduate schools of social work, found the social policy makers disparaging casework, and the casework faculty disparaging other methods.

There may be no other profession that is attempting to organize such diverse, far-flung, loosely related activities, tasks and skills as social work. It is the very breadth of social work's concern that contributes to the practice-education difficulties. Perhaps there is a relationship between the streetcorner worker in a slum neighborhood and a community chest budget director, between an activity director in a home for the aged and a public assistance intake worker, between a worker carrying cases in an intensive treatment center for disturbed children and a worker helping to organize the poor in a Community Action Program. But finding that relationship and developing a common 2-year curriculum that will prepare them for their jobs is a Herculean task—perhaps an impossible one.

FALLACY OF THE CONCEPT OF GENERIC EDUCATION

This paper is not the place for an extended discussion of the concept of the generic emphasis in social work education. But I wish to state my belief that to the degree that social work education has committed itself to the concept of generic education, it has weakened its articulation with the various fields of practice.

The development of a generic curriculum was a necessary stage in developing a cohesive plan of social work education. It has served to identify the elements that are common to all social work practice and was essential in the effort to define the profession of social work itself. Although it was a positive step in the history of social work education, I think it is fruitless to continue to pursue this course exclusively. The whole concept of "the generic" must be reexamined lest it become a coverup for failure to explore the limitations of present social work education and a cloak to conceal the absence of major knowledge areas in the education of social workers. In an insightful article, Harriet M. Bartlett[4] has pointed out that "in order to practice competently in a specific field, there is more to be learned in the way of deeper knowledge and new methods [not taught in the school] than can be acquired through job experience alone." She goes on to state, "It is in fact possible that the major difference between the fields of practice will eventually be in deeper knowledge about specific life situations and areas of social functioning that each requires of practice and contributes back to the social work profession."

For too long schools have taken the attitude that whatever is not part of the school curriculum can be easily learned on the job. The knowledge base that is different in the various fields, and the way in which that knowledge is to be obtained, have been largely ignored. I do not believe it is sufficient, as Bartlett suggests, that "they [the students] should be helped to develop a sense of responsibility for mastering the additional knowledge and skill required for competent practice in each field." This places upon the practice agencies the unreasonable demand of making up for educational lacks.

Agencies may not have communicated effectively to the schools what is unsatisfactory about the latters' training. Too frequently agencies have talked about a lack of knowledge of the specifics of their particular field in terms of the kinds of information that can be learned through practice. Perhaps the agencies have not identified clearly enough the knowledge base that is required.

When an adoption agency, for example, complains that new graduates do not know anything about adoption, they have not said enough; when they state that the student's knowledge of genetics, child development, anthropology and sociology are insufficient to enable him to work with unmarried mothers, to understand medical and psychological evaluations of a child and to appraise adoption standards, they are making a criticism of the student's preparation that cannot be easily overcome in the agency's setting through repeated practice of inservice training. With one-third of the graduates of schools of social work employed in child welfare settings, it is not unreasonable for child welfare agencies to demand that the schools' graduates be better equipped with knowledge that will prepare them to function adequately in a child welfare agency.

Such knowledge cannot be "generic." A worker in a child welfare agency should have a thorough knowledge of child development. A social worker employed by the Veteran's Administration has less use for such a background. The knowledge base required for a social worker going into youth recreation work is quite different from that of a specialist in work with the aged.

UNDUE EMPHASIS ON THERAPY

A further source of dissatisfaction with the current educational effort is the definition of casework that seems to exist in some schools. To the degree that casework seems to be equated with therapy, the schools are graduating many ill equipped students. Of course, some individualized service agencies that conceive of their function as essentially therapy are content with this emphasis. But for a wide range of other agencies, including many of the newest ones, this emphasis does not equip the new graduate for work. Most poverty-oriented agencies, for example, do not see therapy as an effective tool in their job. An intensive "therapeutic casework" approach is not needed for effective supportive casework in a public assistance agency. Most graduates require not only additional education but reeducation to reverse attitudes in order to work effectively in a child protective agency or other "aggressive casework" agencies. Frequently when new graduates are told that foster parents or child care staff are not casework clients and that workers do not have a "casework relationship" with them, they are utterly confused. They see themselves as therapists, not as social workers with skills that enable them to work at many different levels with a wide variety of persons.

Certainly, generic education has so far failed the field of practice in producing administrators, social planners and so-called community organizers. Eveline Burns stated recently: "First, the attempt to pursue that will-o'-the-wisp, 'generic social work,' ought to be abandoned. As the tasks to be performed in the areas delineated are considered—identification of commonly experienced but unmet needs and invention of ways in which they might be met; evaluation of policies and programs; and social planning—it is difficult to see what there is in common between the practitioner in this area, and the case or group worker. A common philosophy, yes; a central preoccupation with what happens to people, yes; a common historical background, yes. Beyond this, it is difficult to see anything generic. The behavioral and social science basis on which both groups should draw very quickly becomes highly differentiated. The skills required are different. Even the personal qualities that make for success in one or the other field of endeavor are different."[5]

I agree that the social planner and the administrator are "different breeds of cat." In my view, the student cannot obtain the knowledge that he needs for these functions in the 2-year course of a graduate school of social work. Nor do I believe that it is educationally sound for him to consume half of his educational time in field work. There should be much more emphasis upon academic study in preparation for jobs in administration, community organization and social policy development.

As it stands now, the person entering administration in social work is half prepared. In most instances, his knowledge of anything beyond groupwork or casework is extremely limited. Whether he succeeds or fails depends more on his personality, personal interest and self-education than on his social work education. Practice is very seriously handicapped by lack of well prepared administrators and policy makers, and the administration of agencies is sorely weakened. Many administrators know little about economics, less about administration, little about the interaction of various power groups in our pluralistic society. They are uninformed and uninterested in the sources of funding public and private agencies; they are inept in working with boards of directors and public officials, poorly equipped to organize supporting groups, including volunteers. Most importantly, they remain frustrated caseworkers or group workers who fill administrative and policy positions simply because there is no one else to do so.

Community organizers and planners are needed in the top echelons of direct-service agencies, not just in fund-raising and planning agencies alone. It is little wonder, therefore, that public welfare agencies are for the most part administered by nonsocial workers and that the most common accusation against both private and public agencies is that they have stagnated in terms of devising imaginative new functions, policies or methods.

Burns believes there should be two distinct types of professional worker: One would be concerned with bringing about change in the individual; and the second would be concerned with bringing about change in social institutions. I would add another category to differentiate between approaches for bringing about change in the individual.

Despite new developments in some schools, too much of social work education produces people whose primary concept of their function in effecting change in the individual is treatment of pathology. This is one of the major reasons, in my opinion, for the widespread rejection of social work as a major professional partner in the poverty programs. Many professional leaders of other disciplines—psychology, anthropology, education, etc.—see hope for the poor in approaches that emphasize human development, cognitive development, improved social organization and cooperative self-help. These are approaches that emphasize the innate strength in human beings, their potential for growth, for education. It is ironic, in view of early social work history and philosophy, that social work in its orientation to pathology is frequently seen as representing the antithesis of these concepts. Thus, there is a search for a new discipline to do essentially what social work was created to do. Social work education should continue to develop and teach casework methods; it should continue to be interested in rehabilitation and therapy for the individual beset with pathology. However, it must rid itself of its apparent conviction that therapeutic casework is the basic method of social work. Human development, social adjustment, institutional change, social planning and organization must have an equal emphasis if social work is to achieve its historic purpose.

I do not mean to suggest that the present state of affairs can be laid entirely at the door of the schools. It is equally the product of practice. In agencies the most commonly heard complaint is that faculty is not "up" on current practice and its problems; conversely, in schools, the complaint is that practitioners are unaware of current philosophy in social work education. The Council on Social Work Education has played a major role in attempting to reduce the validity of these complaints.

LIMITATIONS OF FIELD INSTRUCTION SETTINGS

Field instruction is the part of the curriculum that links practice to education. For it to be of high quality, it must take place in practice settings that are the best that agencies can offer. However, field instruction now takes place in many substandard agencies, so that the school brings the practice methods to the agencies, not the reverse. Field instruction also takes place in innovative settings in which the major purpose may be to develop new clusters of services or systems for the delivery of service. There learning tends to focus on the goal of the systems rather than on methods through which the systems are achieved. In some field settings, students are the major purveyors of service, so that giving service takes precedence over learning, and quality of service becomes questionable. Also, to the degree that the field instruction unit is isolated from the host agency, that unit rather than the field of practice becomes the major source of feedback to the schools for testing, refinement and development of practice.

"The Manual of Accrediting Standards" of the Council on Social Work Education (Appendix II, Criterion 4) states: "The agency should be in good standing in the community and in the profession. It should qualify for membership in those standard-setting bodies, national and local, appropriate to its field of service." Quite properly, the Standards state that an agency should qualify, not that it should belong. For I do not think it appropriate for any group to require an agency to hold membership in one of the national standard-setting agencies.

How many schools of social work try to ascertain from national accrediting bodies whether an agency used for field work meets its standards? Inquiry of several national accrediting bodies indicates that such inquiries are almost nonexistent.

In my view—which, given my job, could admittedly be biased—this standard is an extremely important one in developing ways for better communication between the schools and agencies. If, as so frequently happens out of necessity, students are placed by schools in agencies for which the schools have little respect, bridging the gap between practice and education becomes almost impossible. The number of faculty in charge of field placements who are unaware of the standards of national agencies is legion. They either are substituting their own judgment or have given up in desperation of ever seeing standards met.

Until some better accrediting method is determined, I would suggest that the schools have a responsibility to become much better acquainted with the standards of the present accrediting bodies, and to interact with them in assessing of agencies.

Individual faculty members have participated in the standard-setting committees of various national agencies. They are active in planning conferences, frequently give seminars, speeches and consultation to both local agencies and national standard-setting bodies, serve on editorial boards, and work on committees for the development of teaching materials. They frequently work on committees that help state departments establish standards for licensing. They participate in community surveys. Rarely, however, have I known of a school of social work as a whole that was actively and meaningfully engaged in upgrading the standards of the agencies in which it placed students.

THE USE OF PROFESSIONAL WORKERS

Accrediting standards often set a minimum, but never a maximum, on the percentage of fully trained staff employed. Yet from the standpoint of freeing social workers for new fields of practice, for teaching and for manning new services, it is vital that we make sure that no practice agency has more professional social workers than it needs. The schools and the national accrediting agencies could assist the profession by studying the question of misuse of professional manpower. It is a poor educational experience for students in their field instruction to observe professional workers carrying out functions that are inappropriate to their education and training. Meaningful accrediting of agencies in which students are placed is an extremely important function for both the field of practice and the field of education, and must be stepped up, with greater sanctions and visibility.

The principal point at which social work education inevitably comes into contact with practice is in field instruction, this time-honored, though debatable method of education. It is here that it is frequently determined how much faculty knows about agencies and how much agencies know about education. Too frequently the only contact between the agency and the school is with the field instruction supervisor. Agency administrators must invest much more time in liaison with the schools.

AGENCY OBSERVATIONS ON EDUCATION

Among observations of agency executives about social work education are some that may seem impertinent:

1) Agencies believe schools are lax in the rigor of education in field and classroom. Many believe that the lack of rigor is designed less for the interests of the student than for the convenience of the faculty.

2) The cost to agencies of field instruction is becoming a more and more pressing problem, as agency administrators and boards have become more attuned to cost analysis.

3) Agencies believe there should be a year-round commitment of students because regardless of theory, students do carry caseloads. When those caseloads are left at the end of the 8-month training period, not only does the agency have a logistical problem in the covering of cases, but the needs of the clients may suffer. Clients are not served for the sake of education. It is not possible for agencies in many settings, including child welfare, to select cases for students that can be arbitrarily dropped by the student at the end of the spring term. However, cases are frequently closed regardless of the needs of the client. One graduate school operated a neighborhood center staffed entirely by students and faculty. It closed the center during the summer, the time of greatest need for this type of service.

NEW EDUCATION-PRACTICE RELATIONSHIPS

I very much favor the development of the kind of school-administered, year-round service agency that is taking place in some schools. I think a great deal will be accomplished in the education of faculty on current methods of practice, providing a way is found to make certain that the school-run agencies are cognizant of the best standards in the field. It will be interesting to see if the agencies that the schools develop take Criterion 4 to heart and obtain accrediting by one of the present accrediting bodies, or whether they assume this to be unnecessary.

Another development that I think will contribute to better agency-school articulation is joint faculty-agency appointments. Such dual appointments might well help to bridge the knowledge gap that both schools and agencies maintain exists. Agency concern that faculty have little current knowledge about practice, and school concern that executives and practitioners are not au courant with current educational philosophy might be overcome if there were this opportunity for constant feedback.

Social work has before it a great opportunity to form a systematic interrelationship between practice and education. Agencies and schools can work together to develop sound models for the utilization of the team approach, involving the fully qualified social workers and subprofessionals, technicians and volunteers. There is no thinking person in the profession who believes that it is possible or desirable to fill all jobs in social work with holders of master's degrees. How these various levels of personnel are to share responsibilities and work together is the most pressing problem facing practice. So far there has been much talk and little action. The job cannot be accomplished unless social work education and practice work together.

I believe that, if this important task is approached realistically, both practice and the schools may be faced with some very unpleasant facts. It may well be, for example, that it will be difficult to ascertain the differences in functioning, or rather in the results of the functioning, of a master's degree social worker and one with only an undergraduate college degree. It may turn out that differences in effective practice correlate only with length and type of practice experience rather than formal graduate school education. It could develop that, instead of practice demanding that education be shortened, social work, like psychology, will have to consider the doctorate, or at least 3 years of graduate education, as the qualifying degree of the professional social worker.

I believe that we will not meet our manpower problems by watering down, shortening or in some other way restricting the knowledge base of the professional social worker. The manpower problem must be met essentially through the development of technicians and subprofessionals. It seems logical to me to intensify the education of the professional social worker, to really establish that the distinction between a professional social worker and one without a graduate degree constitutes a real difference in functioning capacity.

In such an examination, we certainly may discover that many jobs now thought of as social work jobs have few if any components that require graduate social work education. For example, unless the determination of eligibility for financial assistance is divorced from the service program, there may be little excuse for utilizing master's degree social workers except in administration in this largest of all social work programs. It may be that the reason that public assistance programs have been unable to attract social workers is simply because most such jobs do not justify having a social worker.

Some agency executives would like to see schools of social work assume responsibility for more staff development and inservice training. Others object on the basis that scarce teaching personnel should be reserved for teaching master's degree students and for providing consultation to programs of staff development. Regardless of the controversy, logic suggests that serving as a consultant or teacher in staff development programs will promote school-agency understanding.

It is my view that practice and education—especially practice—will be most benefited if schools continue to concentrate on the formal training of social work manpower rather than dissipating their energies at this time in conducting extensive on-the-job training programs. Certainly, there is a place and a necessity for educators—experts in pedagogy—to assist as consultants in these areas. But the greatest need in social work is to strengthen the significance and relevance of formal social work education.

This is the basic question facing all of social work today: In view of the times in which we live, is what we are doing significant and relevant?

Fortunately, what I have to say is in part already redundant comment for many schools of social work and agencies. Several schools, including Michigan State, are planning or operating full year programs. Washington University and the University of Washington are becoming major forces in community planning in their states. Arizona is actively engaged in upgrading standards of agencies within the state in cooperation with national agencies. The University of Southern California and San Diego State University are experimenting with eliminating the traditional divisions among casework, group work and community organization. Several schools are developing a reputation for specialization in a field of practice. Others are engaged in putting casework in its proper perspective and developing a rich curriculum in social planning and community organization. Research projects and joint school-agency projects examining multicareer lines are not uncommon. Family agencies, settlement houses and a host of other agencies are reshaping their methods by active involvement in poverty programs. The doctoral program in many schools is upgrading the quality of all social planning and social innovation. And many schools and practice agencies are joining together in a common realization that a separation between the "knowers" and the "doers" can produce only chaos.

REFERENCES

1. Official statement of Curriculum Policy, No. 61–91–15RN, Council on Social Work Education, July 30, 1962.

2. Remarks by John W. Gardner, Secretary of Health, Education, and Welfare. *Journal of Education of Social Work,* II, 1 (spring 1966), p. 5.

3. Getting Into Social Work, *Mademoiselle* (January 1966).

4. Harriet M. Bartlett. "The Place and Use of Knowledge in Social Work Practice," *Social Work,* IX (July 1964), p. 36.

5. Eveline M. Burns. "Tomorrow's Social Needs and Social Work Education," *Journal of Education for Social Work,* II, 1 (spring 1966), p. 10.

OTHER PUBLICATIONS OF JOSEPH H. REID

Evaluation of Ten Years' Work With Emotionally Disturbed Children. (With Lillian J. Johnson.) Seattle: Ryther Child Center, 1947, 19 pp.

Hope for Three Out of Four. (With Lillian J. Johnson.) *Survey,* October 1947, LXXXIII.

Residential Treatment Centers for Emotionally Disturbed Children: A Descriptive Study. (With Helen R. Hagan.) New York: Child Welfare of America, 1952, 310 pp.

New Emphases at the Child Welfare League. *Children,* November-December 1955, II, 6, pp. 222–226.

Trends Toward Better Children's Services. *Child Welfare,* May 1955, XXXIV, 5, pp. 1–16.

Ensuring Adoption for Hard-to-Place Children. *Child Welfare,* March 1956, XXXV, 3, pp. 4–8.

Principles, Values, and Assumptions Underlying Adoption Practice. *Social Work,* January 1957, II, 1, pp. 22–29. Also in: *Readings in Adoption,* edited by I. Evelyn Smith. New York Philosophical Library, 1963, pp. 26–38.

Administrative Auspices of Residential Treatment. *Child Welfare,* March 1958, XXXVII, 3, pp. 5–17.

Is All Well With the American Family? *The Social Welfare Forum.* Official Proceedings of the 1958 National Conference of Social Welfare. New York: Columbia University Press, 1958, pp. 104–144.

Homemaker Service for Children. *Children,* November-December 1958, V, 6, pp. 210–216.

Action Called For—Recommendations, in *Children in Need of Parents,* by Henry S. Maas and Richard E. Engler, Jr. New York: Columbia University Press, 1959, pp. 378–397.

Discussion of the Socially Handicapped Child, in *Proceedings of the Second Mississippi Conference on Handicapped Children.* February 22–23, 1961, Jackson, Miss., pp. 70–78.

Social Services for Children and Youth. (With Leonard W. Mayo.) *Children,* March-April 1962, IX, 2, pp. 66–72.

The Emotion and Logic of Structure. *Child Welfare,* November 1962, XLI, 9, pp. 477–483.

The Case for Day Care, in *Helping the Family in Urban Society,* edited by Fred Delliquadri. Selected papers from the 1962 National Conference on Social Welfare. New York: Columbia University Press, 1963, pp. 79–95.

Some Observations on Local Agencies and Federations. *Child Welfare,* December 1963, XLII, 10, pp. 493–494.

America's Forgotten Children. Guest editorial, *Parents' Magazine,* February 1966.

Legislation for Day Care, in *Preliminary Report of a Consultation on Working Women and Day Care Needs,* June 1, 1967, Washington, D.C. U.S. Women's Bureau, 1967, pp. 14–19.

The Role of Social Work in Meeting Child Welfare Needs in the Urban Crisis, in *The New Face of Social Work,* proceedings of an institute sponsored by the Spence Chapin Adoption Service, October 18, 1968, New York, pp. 14–20.

Untitled paper in *Unmarried Parents and Their Children: Trends, Challenges, Concerns.* Symposium in honor of Florence Kreech on her 20th anniversary as Executive Director of Louise Wise Services, October 30, 1969, New York, pp. 5–12.

Child Welfare in Urban Conditions. *International Child Welfare Review,* January 1970, 5–6, pp. 75–78.

Day Care Services: Our Best Investment for the Future. Guest editorial, *Parents' Magazine,* April 1970.

"A National Child Welfare Policy." *Proceedings of the Australian Child Care Conference,* 1972, Monash University, Melbourne, February 20–25, pp. 1–10.

Child Welfare Since 1912. (With Maxine Phillips.) *Children Today,* March-April 1972, I, 2, pp. 13–18.

"Day Care: Crisis of Conscience." *Lutheran Social Concern,* XII, 1, spring 1972, pp. 51–54.

On "Deinstitutionalization," *Child Welfare,* April 1975, LIV, 4, pp. 295–297.

"The Role of the Voluntary Sector." A response to "A Framework for Public-Voluntary Collaboration in the Social Services," by Alfred J. Kahn. *The Social Welfare Forum,* 1976. Official Proceedings 103d Annual Forum, National Conference on Social Welfare, Washington, D.C. June 13–17, 1976. New York: Columbia University Press, 1977, pp. 63–69.